How to be a Sports Agent

www.highstakespublishing.com

By the same author

How to Complain

How to be a
Sports Agent

Mel Stein

High Stakes

This edition published in 2008 by High Stakes Publishing
21 Great Ormond Street, London, WC1N 3JB
www.highstakespublishing.com

Editor: Richard Howard

Previously published as *How to Succeed as a Sports Agent* –
this edition significantly updated.

ISBN: 978-84344 045 1

6 8 10 9 7 5

Typeset by Windrush Publishing Services, Gloucestershire
Printed in Great Britain by Clays Ltd, St Ives plc

For all those players who stayed loyal to me
throughout their careers and
in particular JG, RC, JO and CB

Acknowledgements

With thanks to Mark Levinstein for providing the extra material relevant to the United States.

Contents

Introduction

We are agents, we are agents,
No one likes us, we don't care.

A sad refrain, but an accurate one. Even I, after writing a book as to how to succeed as one, always veer away from the nametag of 'agent'.

'How shall we describe you?' they ask, whenever I make a media appearance. 'Sports agent?'

'No,' I say as an automatic response. 'Sports lawyer', or as The FA would now have me designated 'Registered Lawyer'.

And indeed, I've started so many conversations with potential clients by saying,

'I'm not an agent, I'm a solicitor.'

Now you could equally appositely sing,

We are lawyers. We are lawyers.
No one likes us, we don't care.

But this isn't a book about how to succeed as a solicitor (though there's an idea!). It's about how to be a successful sports agent. And, I suppose, how to achieve that in an ethical way so that sports agency can be regarded as a profession of which one can be proud to be a member.

That is going to be some challenge. Perhaps, when I've finished I'll read the book myself and you will see on your screens those magic words, 'Mel Stein, Sports Agent'.

A lot of water has flowed under the bridge since the first two editions of this book were published. Transfer fees in professional football have risen astronomically, largely due to the desire of Chelsea's owner to purchase any player any potential rival could possibly want. But other clubs have joined in the chase for glory to push salaries in the Premiership to new heights. And now we have the new FA Agents Regulations with which to contend and to which I will simply refer from here on in as The FA Regulations. It was difficult before them to be an agent specialising in football clients, but now it has been made doubly difficult. I was going to say well-nigh impossible but that might have discouraged wannabe football agents from reading any further or even, if word of mouth got out, to kill the sales of this book stone dead in the water.

It was Dave Nightingale writing in the United States for *The Sporting News* some years ago, who cynically said, 'Want to be an agent? Open your mouth and declare yourself one. You don't need a law degree or a certified public accountant's shingle. You don't need an education, you don't have to have a licence... a knowledge of sport is preferable but not mandatory. All you have to do is convince some professional athlete or would-be pro that you can get a better deal for them from their employer than they could get for themselves. Voilà! You are a member of one of the world's newest professions.'

But is that right? Maybe you don't need a law degree, but FIFA, the world's governing body of football (that's soccer for anybody in the States picking up this volume and thumbing through – well, at least you understood 'accountant's shingle'!) does accept that a qualified lawyer doesn't need to be licensed, although, as you will see later, The FA does not agree. However, as for everybody else, licensing regulations haven't taken too long to start wrapping their tentacles around the world's newest profession, not just in football but in many other sports as well. Indeed, in football, more people fail the licensing exam now than pass, so at least that's a start.

In its simplest form, an agent is a representative of a principal, i.e. an agent is an individual or a company who represents a sportsperson. They try to get them a better contract; a better endorsement; a better sponsorship; a better deal. Nothing wrong with that, is there? Or is there? Many of my journalistic 'friends' think there is. Just read Patrick Collins in *The Mail on Sunday* for one. Actually, don't bother. He never writes anything nice about anybody – me in particular.

But this is not a book about how to hate journalists. If you ever get to represent a high-profile player you won't need a book for that, it will just come naturally. This is a book not just about how to succeed, but how to remain successful and, at the same time, deal always in your clients' interests. The problem there lies in the conflict between the interests of the agent and the interests of the principal (i.e. the sportsperson). When a lawyer represents a client, then the interests of the client are paramount. The lawyers' governing body says so. If a solicitor puts his own interests first, then The Solicitors Regulation Authority in the United Kingdom will deal with him (or her... no need to be sexist about this, as many female solicitors as male are subject to disciplinary proceedings) accordingly and, if necessary, will strike him, or her, off. Yet all too often a small number of agents of sportspeople are concerned with their commissions first and their clients second. And I hope you noticed how I subtly shifted away from disciplinary proceedings against lady lawyers. I want children to be able to read this book and say:

'Daddy, when I grow up I want to be a sports agent.'

Back to the business in hand. Surely if the client's income is maximised then it must follow that the agent's commission must similarly rise. This ignores the one factor that must make every athlete tremble in their designer tracksuit – human greed. If an employer makes £1,000,000 available to a sportsperson and an agent takes 10% then they'll earn £100,000, leaving their client with £900,000. However, if the agent persuades the club to pay them £200,000 (which as we'll see later is a breach of The FA Regulations) then suddenly their client is left with a miserly £800,000. What, no tears for the athlete who has to struggle through on a sum in excess of three-quarters of a million?

But that is part of the problem too. There is so much money sloshing around in professional sport today that the wrong people are being enticed into sport to act as representatives. So maybe the title of this book should be *How to be a Good Sports Agent* or *How to be an Honest Sports Agent* or, better still, *How to be a Good Honest Sports Agent*.

That is what I will be aiming to do. To show you how to keep the balance, to do the best for your client and still earn enough money for yourself. To find a way through the minefields of regulations created by the various governing bodies of sports. Greed is not good but making money for yourself in a honest and ethical way is not bad either.

The Licence

When Dave Nightingale said that an agent didn't need a licence he was talking about more innocent times. Nowadays several major sports in this country, throughout Europe and in the States, have a licensing system. Until March 2001, certainly as far as football was concerned, getting a licence didn't mean being qualified. Basically, provided you had enough money to post the security bond, hadn't murdered anybody (or at least nobody of any note) or were able to con your way through the easiest of interviews, then the Football Association (FA) would grant you a licence. Whether that was a domestic licence (enabling you solely to negotiate transfers in England) or a full FIFA licence (permitting you to deal abroad), merely depended upon the amount of the bond.

From 1 March 2001, the Players' Agents' Regulations came into force for people who want to represent footballers. These were replaced by the 1st January 2007 Regulations and these were so successful (not) that The FA introduced The FA Regulations in September 2007 and these really bit for the first time during the January 2008 Transfer Window.

If you are planning to set up a sports agency in the UK, then the odds are that you will be planning to represent, *inter alia*, professional footballers. That's where the real money lies in this country and although there are agents out there who are making a good living from acting for golfers, rugby players, boxers, cricketers and tennis stars, there are only a few who limit themselves to one sport representation. If that's what you intend to do, then obviously your first port of call as far as the requirements for licensing are concerned is the appropriate governing body of the relevant sport (the Rugby Football Union for rugby, Lawn Tennis Association for tennis, England and Wales Cricket Board for cricket – never understood the Welsh bit unless it is meant to apply solely to Glamorgan) the Football Association for football or the relevant international board or association. As far as the USA is concerned my good friend Mark Levinstein, a DC-based sports lawyer who worked with me in jointly representing the US National Soccer team back in 1994 and still represents them in their negotiations with the USSF (United States Soccer Federation) has written a couple of chapters for this edition which contains the basic information.

In athletics, if you want to be a race agent and be entitled to enter your clients for races under the auspices of the International Amateur Athletics Federation (IAAF), you have to be licensed. But to be licensed you have to show you have some experience, but because you can't get the experience without being licensed this has inevitably led to licences generally being granted to ex-athletes. More and more agencies are setting up athletics divisions run by athletes just to get the necessary licence and, since some of those agencies have been firmly rooted in the world of football, you can bet your bottom dollar that they'll soon be squeezing the sport dry right down to its squeaky financial pips. But more about these non-soccer sports later.

The FA Regulations and any updates are available from the Football Association (and are available on their website at www.the-fa.org) and although they kindly gave me permission to reproduce them in the Appendices to this book (which is more than generous considering the grief I have given them over the development of the Regulations and the considerable legal costs they have incurred), I (and my publishers) decided the book would be better, shorter and cheaper if the reader simply referred to them on The FA's website in conjunction with this

book. I have devoted a whole chapter to an overview of The FA
Regulations as they now stand because unless you understand
them and comply with them then you're agency career as far
as football is concerned is doomed to failure. At this stage I am
only looking at the licensing aspects and regulations.

Appendix IX sets out the rules for obtaining a licence. As The
FA Regulations say that for the purposes of transfers players
may only use the services of an Authorised Agent you may as
well skip right along to getting the magic document. There used
to be some exceptions to the rule of not being able to represent
a player without a licence. A parent could act for a child, a
brother for a brother, a wife for a husband (and there are several
footballers' wives whose forceful personalities would make
them formidable agents indeed). There is an apocryphal (or
perhaps not so apocryphal) story of one particular footballer's
wife being physically ejected from the dressing room by the
manager when she tried to renegotiate her husband's deal
there and then. Nothing seems to permit the representation
of a father by a son! However, the regulations don't say that
a manager or coach has to be represented by a licensed agent.
To bring almost everybody who might represent a footballer
under their jurisdiction (with the exception of the family cat)
The FA has introduced several classes of representatives all
classed under the all-inclusive banner of 'Authorised Agents'.
These include, Licensed Agents, Registered Agents, Registered
Lawyers, Registered Overseas Agents and Registered Close
Relations. This latter class is now to be extended to parents,
guardians, persons with parental responsibility, siblings and
spouses. Interestingly enough, none of these can receive any
payment for their advice from the player or from any third
party. It will be interesting to see how they enforce that one
when a grateful son buys his dad an expensive car as a thank
you for his help in getting him a contract worth £10,000 per
week!

Before The FA began its current tinkering, the main relevant
exception (at least as far as I was concerned) related to
lawyers, as previously touched upon. However under The FA

Regulations all that has changed. Previously, all a lawyer had to do to be able to represent a footballer was to be 'legally authorised to practise as a lawyer in compliance with the rules in force in their country of domicile'. So a South African lawyer domiciled there but living in the UK did not need a licence but, on the strict interpretation of the rule, if you were a lawyer who was qualified in your home country and had abandoned your domicile before being qualified in the country of your adopted domicile, you did need to be licensed. Under The FA Regulations if you are a Scottish lawyer who has registered in Scotland you will have to re-register before you can work under the auspices of The FA. Curiously, FIFA takes a different stance and continues to maintain under their January 2008 Regulations that lawyers are exempt. Make of that what you will, but I'm not quite finished on arguing that one even though The Solicitors' Regulatory Authority (SRA) seem to have given up the fight.

The same applies to the documentation between the Exempt Individual/Agent and the player. Until now, all a lawyer needed to do was to rely upon his Law Society-approved form Retainer Letter. Now, as they would only be able to operate within the Regulations, they would need to have the player enter into the standard form of representative agreement. This just doesn't seem right to me. The SRA regulates lawyers and I really don't see why we should submit to a double regulation via The FA. I am assured that registration by a lawyer to become a 'Registered Agent' is a mere formality, but the catch is that the registration itself will submit lawyers to double regulation, by their own professional bodies and The Football Association.

There was a recent interesting case regarding Preston North End where, in all good faith, they negotiated with a player's designated representative who was with a Channel Island law firm. It transpired that the individual 'put into bat' by the firm was not a qualified solicitor, though he was fully supervised by a partner. Notwithstanding that, the Football Association in their wisdom chose to fine Preston £1,000 for using the services of an unlicensed individual.

I, and most leading sports lawyers, still believe the current FA Regulations to be anti-competitive or a restraint of trade in old-fashioned legal terms. As I mentioned above Solicitors are regulated by SRA and should not need to submit themselves to a parallel regulatory body in the form of The Football Association. I did say in the last edition of this book that if nothing else the outcome might at least justify a third edition of this book! Thank you FA for the fertile material you provide to me for lectures and publications.

In order to be a football agent then pursuant to Appendix II you have to be a 'natural person' and, in addition, a European Union national, or be domiciled in England or having lived here for two years prior to application. Something may have got lost in the translation here, but what it means is that a company or a partnership can't get a licence. Two partners in a firm means you need two licences. If you carry on your business through a corporation then everybody who negotiates contracts for the company and its clients has to be licensed. The Association of Sports Agents has been formed which has been recognised as a meaningful voice within the industry and one of its aims is to lobby for Corporate Licences.

By the way, as I interpret the rules you do not have to be licensed to represent a footballer on his commercial matters, but such representation does, now, for the first time impact upon your total freedom to represent him (or any third party) in relation to football contracts etc. The absurdity of this is that there are no regulations governing somebody's right to negotiate a £10m sponsorship deal but you would have had to jump through several hoops to deal with Wrexham with regard to a contract worth £500 per week. Sorry, Wrexham, you may well be paying kings' ransoms to your players (though I don't think so) but you were the first name that sprang to mind.

One rule which should have the casual observer rolling on their back with their legs kicking up in the air is that each applicant under Article 1.2 must 'fulfil the requirements of a test of good character and reputation'. The FA are entitled to consider his criminal record and financial history and 'any history of dealings by The Applicant in relation to the game of football or otherwise which The Association may consider relevant to his acceptability'. This is a bit of an example of closing the stable door after the horse is in the next county but one, given that at least one undischarged bankrupt was granted a licence by the English FA, and there is no question of making existing licence holders apply again. However, The FA does make it clear that anybody applying who has acted as an Unauthorised Agent in the two years up to application will be rejected. So be warned. Don't try to be clever and act for players before you have your licence and as we will see later 'acting for players' has a very wide interpretation.

A Licensed Agent can't hold any position with a club although, from the way some managers guide players towards designated agents, they might just as well be the agents themselves. Without in any way suggesting any impropriety, it is not a perfect situation where certain managers have their sons or brothers working for agencies or even establishing agencies themselves. Personally, I believe the rules should be extended so there can be no relationship whatsoever between anybody at a football club and a licensed agent or, if there is, that particular licensed agent should be barred from conducting any business within or on behalf of that club with perhaps the only exception being minimal shareholding in publicly quoted agencies. The FA Regulations do go further in this respect than they have gone before but are hardly draconian.

However, even if you get rejected by your National Association (The FA as far as England is concerned), don't despair because you can appeal to FIFA. If FIFA doesn't love you either, then I am afraid you have to wait two years before you can apply again. Sitting written exams twice a year has been introduced into the new rules. These will be held on identical dates throughout the world (presumably to stop cheating – although no one seems to have addressed the issue of different time zones). Even if you pass the initial form-filling and good character test and scrape through the exam (which was initially multiple choice but has since become considerably harder) you still have to complete payment for a professional liability insurance, which must be lodged with the relevant national association and these have to meet the requirements of FIFA as decided from time to time.

The old Article 7 was quite extraordinary because it stated that if the agent couldn't get insurance cover (and the only likely reasons would be a bad claims record, dishonesty or something nasty in their particular woodshed), then they could give a guarantee for a hundred thousand Swiss Francs. The logic of this escaped me as this sum of money was hardly likely to be adequate compensation for negligence or dishonesty against the background of the sort of level of figures now involved in professional football around the world. Clearly, for once, The FA agreed with me because now it's no insurance, no licence.

Once you have been licensed, you have to adhere to a code of professional conduct (which is part of the Players' Agents' Regulations now set out in Appendix IV. Once you have read this and once more resumed a vertical position after the hysterical laughter to which I am sure you will succumb, you will see that FA have pinpointed just about everything that a disreputable sports agent (and I believe there are more than a few of those around) might do and notwithstanding The FA Regulations I believe will continue to do. Leopards don't change their spots just because there are big game hunters in the jungle.

You have to perform your occupation conscientiously (well, see my reference to hidden commission earlier) and to conduct yourself in a manner 'worthy of respect and befitting his profession'. You must adhere to 'truth, clarity and objectivity'. Now, many sports agents wouldn't know the truth if it steamrollered them into the ground whilst at the same time spelling out the word in scarlet letters ten feet tall. But this book, don't forget, is about how to be a good, honest sports agent, so my advice is, never lie. Always tell the truth, however unpalatable it might be.

If your client has been told by some unscrupulous agency that if they sign with them (and them alone) they can get them into one of the top five Premiership clubs but you know they are just about ready for the Reserves of a Conference League side, then tell them so. They may leave but when their new agent hasn't come through with the goods, then there is a reasonable chance they'll be coming back, crawling on their hands and knees, assuming you still want to try to work for them.

If you get your licence, don't forget that it is personal and non-transferable but, on the plus side, you do get your name on The FA's official website. How you go about setting up or expanding your business, I will deal with later but for now all you need to remember is that you must have a written contract with all your clients. There is a standard FIFA contract which in my view is totally insufficient to safeguard any agent. There is also now a standard FA agreement which also needs some work on it although the amendments you can make to it are limited and some terms are compulsory. With regard to the content of the form of contract I suggest you will just have to hold your breath until you get to Chapter 3. That's what we writers call a cliff-hanger.

The regulations stipulate that only the licensed agent can 'represent and promote the interests of the players and/or clubs with other players and/or clubs'. Any employee's work must be limited to 'administrative duties' and the National Association issuing the licence must be sent a list of employees at least once a year. The FA Regulations do introduce the new definition of 'Connected Agent' and this includes one who is employed by you, co-directors or shareholders in the same organisations, and most controversial of all those 'having any contractual or other arrangement whether formal or informal to co-operate in the provision of any agency services or to share the revenue or profits of any part of their Agency Activities'. This does mean that consultants are now 'connected' and we will see the impact of that when I look at The FA Regulations in detail. For the moment all I will say is that you have to think carefully before entering into any arrangements with any third parties whatsoever (even with regard to commercial contracts) whether they are Authorised Agents under The FA Regulations or not.

The Football Association Agents Regulations 2007

THE DEFINITIONS

Whenever I give a lecture on The FA Regulations (and believe me I've given many a lecture on them) I find it easier to start with The Definitions as although you don't reach these until you get to Appendix I (which is half-way through the document) the earlier parts of the regulations are impossible to understand unless you also fully appreciate the impact of the definitions.

'Agency Activity' which is, not unsurprisingly, the very nub of The Regulations is a very wide definition indeed. This means 'acting in any way and at any time in the capacity of an agent, representative or adviser to a Club or Player, either directly or indirectly, in the negotiation, arrangement, registration or execution of any Transaction [just wait for the definition of that!] or Contract Negotiation other than as a Lawyer who is solely and exclusively undertaking or providing Permitted Legal Advice'.

If there are any lawyers out there reading this who have not been following the development of The FA Regulations with wonder then I bet you are wondering how The FA come to be in the position of deciding what is or isn't 'Permitted Legal Advice'.

Just to put you out of your misery what it means, at least according to The FA, is any advice where the lawyer has a retainer letter, is part of a practice regulated by The SRA and is simply advising on the legal form and legal implications of documents as opposed to negotiating the deal for his client and in particular the financial terms of the deal. So, there you have it. Solicitors, you can't do what you've been doing for clients for years unless you register with The FA. But, it seems you can do it anywhere else in the world where you are operating under The FIFA rules relating to lawyers.

'Person' is defined as being a 'natural person, corporate or unincorporated body (whether or not having separate legal personality) and their personal representatives, successors or permitted assign'. Now that is all a little odd. Only an individual can be a licensed agent but here we have The FA pulling companies into the definition of 'persons'. Believe me, that's not accidental.

They define an 'Agent' as any 'person' who carries out Agency Activity and an 'Authorised Agent' is either a Licensed Agent, a Registered Agent, a Registered Overseas Agent, Registered Close Relations or a Registered Lawyer. Confused yet? You ought to be.

They have sneaked in a definition of 'Commercial Rights' which means any rights 'In relation to a Player arising from the use of the Player's Image or from sponsorship or endorsements or from any other commercial exploitation of rights not directly related to the Player's employment contract'. So that doesn't leave a lot to chance, does it? Silly me. I thought that the job of The FA was to supervise and regulate playing contracts between professional footballers and their clubs and the role of the agent in negotiating those and being paid for it. But here, for the first time we see them going much further and you will see the relevance of this wide definition of 'Commercial Rights' as we proceed.

As if all that was not bad enough they have also introduced a new class of persons, namely the 'Connected Agent'. Now he is somebody who is employed or retained by the same Organisation (I'll get to 'Organisation' in a bit). That's fair enough for 'employed' but a 'retainer' can cover a wealth of things. What if a lawyer is retained by a company to give them legal advice? He is also a Registered Lawyer carrying on a totally independent business of sports management. But once he has been retained to give legal advice to another 'Organisation' he is then connected to that Organisation as far as The FA are concerned. 'Connected' also means where the parties are directors or shareholders or closely related but the real killer is that it also covers parties who have made 'any contractual or other arrangement whether formal or informal to co-operate in the provision of any agency services or to share the revenue or profits of any part of their Agency Activities'. So, if you enlist the help of another agency to place a player and agree to give them a percentage then, even this is only a one-off, as far as The FA are concerned you are 'Connected'. Again, we shall see the effect of this in due course.

They have also widened out the definition of 'Contract Negotiation' far beyond what you or I or any sensible person would consider to be a 'negotiation'. According to them it means 'any negotiation or other related activity, including any communication preparatory to the same the intention or effect of which is *inter alia* to create, terminate or vary the terms of a Player's contract of employment with a Club'. So, if you get one of your team just to phone a club to see if they are interested in a player then that person has triggered off a 'Contract Negotiation'. More of that later.

'Representation agreement' is worth a quick look as this means 'any agreement, arrangement or mandate whether verbal or written, formal or informal', between an Agent, Player or Club which is intended to cover 'the provision of any Agency Activity'. The 'Representation Contract' means a 'representation agreement which must comply with the Obligatory Terms of The Standard Representation Contract'.

Yes, as far as football is concerned at least, they have made my chapters about what should go into the representation contract somewhat redundant because you can't put anything in of which The FA doesn't approve and if they don't approve then you can't register your contract with them and if you don't register it then the club concerned won't deal with you.

Now, before I get onto the actual Regulations themselves are you sure you still want to be a sports agent focussing on football in England?

The Regulations Themselves

As you will have gathered from the definitions in the previous chapter it is not going to be difficult to breach The FA Regulations either deliberately or accidentally. However, if you do almost the first thing the Regulations tell you is that you will be charged with 'Misconduct'. Given that I am supposed to be telling you to be an honest, upstanding agent I can only tell you to comply but I also think it is going to be very hard to comply in full, particularly if you actually want to make a living from this profession. Let's not lose sight of the woods for the trees. There are other sports in which participants can be represented but for the moment I am still sticking to football.

Obviously, it is not just agents to whom The FA Regulations apply. All participants are sucked in, clubs, players and officials alike. Clearly, The FA is trying to ensure that all individuals conducting the business of a football agent within their territory can be regulated by it. Hence its desire to have not just licensed agents but also foreign agents doing business here and lawyers effectively conducting the business of an agent as subject to its regulations. Equally clearly it can't regulate anybody who doesn't sign up to its rules and that, of course, means that anybody who doesn't fall into one of the above categories is an Unauthorised Agent. So, it is hardly surprising that Clause 1 of Regulation A states categorically that neither a club nor a player can directly or indirectly use the services of such a person. What that means to you, presumably as an

Authorised Agent, is that you can't 'front' for an Unauthorised Agent nor can you fee share with him. We'll return to how The FA buttons that one up a little later. Clubs and players do have an obligation to satisfy themselves that the person who is representing them or the individual with whom they are dealing is 'Authorised' so be prepared to provide a copy of your licence to your client and don't be surprised if the club with whom you are negotiating asks to see a copy of your representation agreement and then even checks with The FA to satisfy themselves that you have registered it with them.

As far as the contract itself is concerned I will deal with that in detail in the contract regarding representation and management agreements. But what The FA regulations have done this time around is nailed, once and for all, the concept of duality of representation. Readers of my earlier editions of this book will recall that although you acted for a player even the Inland Revenue recognised that there was an element of service to the club. Clubs were quite happy to pay agents fees on behalf of a player and a player would only be taxed on a proportion of that. Now, Regulation C1 makes it quite clear that an Authorised Agent can only act for one party to a transaction and to ensure that is the case G4 provides that where an agent acts for a player only that player can make the payment. I'll look at that in more depth when I analyse the methodology of payment but enough to say that the effect of this is a killer blow for some of the smaller agents and is likely to push the industry way down below ground again as far as clubs and the more sophisticated agents are concerned.

As if it was not bad enough to stop any kind of recognition of 'duality', The FA has then proceeded to kick the agent when he is down by also saying in C2 that the agent can't act for a club in relation to a player when the agent has carried out any Agency Activity for the player in the last two transfer windows or even just had a representation agreement with him. That is effectively one year. Now you will recall the very wide definition of 'Agency Activity' in the previous chapter and ANY Agency Activity means that you can't 'switch' sides. I can understand

The FA wanting to stop the practice of an agent changing horses from player to club when a transaction is looming just to make sure he gets paid by the club and helps his client avoid paying any tax (or VAT) on a payment that is really his responsibility. What I can't understand is the scenario which has now been created whereby if an agent has an agreement with a player which has come to end, say 11 months earlier, then even if the agent has done nothing for the player in the two preceding years of his contract, even if it was the player's decision not to re-sign, then the agent still can't act for the player's club if they decide to sell him and ask his old agent for help. It simply beggars belief that an inactive representation agreement which the was coming to an end and which, due to circumstances entirely beyond the agent's control, has not been renewed, bars the agent from earning any money from a perfectly legitimate activity within a perfectly legitimate deal.

As if all of that is not enough The FA having kicked the fallen agent now tries to bury him by saying in C2 (c) that if you are a 'Connected Agent' to any Authorised Agent who falls within the above categories that you still can't act for the club. So, if somebody with whom you had any kind of commercial connection had the same spurious connection to the player in question then again you are barred from acting for a potential client with regard to that club. It's pure Alice in Wonderland with the only problem being that The Red Queen, in the shape of The FA, is really beheading people. In fact it is cutting off even more vital parts than the head. Still think you can make a living from being a football agent? OK it's your funeral but please read on. Anybody who has decided to concentrate on golf, rugby or beach volleyball (and I class only the last of these three as a sport) can simply skip the rest of this chapter.

It goes without saying that the restrictions I have set out above also apply in reverse. If you have acted for the club in bringing the player in then for at least 12 months down the line you can't act for the player. I have to say as originally drafted it was much worse, the period of restriction coming down from forever, to five years, to three and now to one. I supposed we ought to be grateful, but, you know what? Actually, we're not. We're all pretty angry and it's still not absolutely clear whether or not this restriction and the one about only the players paying are going to be challenged.

I am sure if there is ever to be a public debate about this The FA will spring to its feet (does it have feet?) and say, 'Ah, but that bloody Stein has failed to mention that you can apply for written authorisation to vary these restrictions'. Yes, you can. Will it be forthcoming? The indication is that it won't and, even if it will, by the time The FA have considered all your representations and have magnanimously agreed you CAN act the transaction will have long passed you by and you will be left clutching a useless piece of paper giving you consent. The FA do say that they have taken on more manpower to deal with all their regulations and to provide speedy resolutions but at the time of writing this is not immediately apparent. Delays of up to two months for them even to register a representation contract are not unknown. Perhaps it will all have improved by the time this book sees the light of day. Perhaps.

If you think it's got as bad as can be then don't believe it. If you have acted for one club in a transaction in relation to a particular player then you can't act for any other club ANYWHERE IN THE WORLD regarding that player for the two transfer window periods. Again, it's not just 'acted for' it's carried out any 'Agency Activity'. And as we've seen that can mean just making a phone call. Once more, the same applies if any Connected Agent has done the same thing. Hopefully, with this book as your guide you'll be really successful and set up your own international network. But if you do so and your partner (or even your vague associate) in Argentina has acted for one club in relation to a player then you can't act for another club in England relating to that player.

Just to put the icing on the cake, or, perhaps more appropriately to hammer the last nail in the coffin of your ambitions, even if you have carried out some commercial activity with regard to the player or the club's or another club's 'Commercial Rights' in any way involving that player or any

Connected party has done so, then, once again, you are well and truly stymied. 'Interest in commercial rights' is also so widely drafted as to be all-encompassing including either direct or indirect interest, beneficial ownership of the commercial rights or any 'contractual or customary arrangement which involves the representation of the player's rights'.

The likelihood is that if you grow as an agent or become part of a larger organisation then you may well have, within the same group of companies, a company that is autonomous and just deals with the commercial rights of clubs and players. Even that can trigger off the sort of restrictions on your free ability to conduct your trade as outlined above.

If you are part of a larger organisation then all the agents in that organisation must act for the same party. Clearly, unlike The SRA and other regulatory bodies The FA has never heard of the concept of 'Chinese walls'. Speaking of organisations, as I have made clear, they are not participants and are not subject to The FA Regulations, The FA gives them no protection but does want to seek some kind of control over them so the sneaky way they do that is by D3, where an agent has to use all reasonable endeavours to ensure that the Organisation for which he works complies with the requirements of The FA regulations. Now if you are as perplexed by that as I am then I am not surprised. Talk about burdens without any benefits!

Regulation E puts even more responsibility on agents, clubs and players insofar as they have to ensure that everybody they deal with obeys the rules. We are one step away from a Police State within the world of football, a State occupied by double agents, grasses and whistle blowers. All I can say, once again, is that for the moment the rules are what they are and however onerous or unfair you or I may consider them then the safe way forward is to work within them and not to give any third party the opportunity to get you into trouble.

I promised to return to remuneration and I am a man of my word. Trust me, I am now not only a lawyer but also an FA Registered Lawyer (albeit under protest). But you will have to wait a little longer until you get to my chapter about what to charge and who pays.

In order to get to the point of being able to charge you have to be able to complete a transaction. You may need help on that and as I've already said you can't seek help from an Unauthorised Agent. But you can seek help from an Authorised Agent provided you can find your way through the maze of regulations that apply to that as well. If you are going to assign or sub-contract an Agency Activity then you have to get the written consent of your client first, then set out the terms of the arrangement in writing and then lodge the document in triplicate with The FA. Again, by the time you've done all that the moment may have passed and quite frankly even as I write this I realise yet again the real problem lies with The FA Regulations. They have been drafted by lawyers and bureaucrats who have no concept of how the football industry really operates. They simply don't work when a transaction is urgent and a player's future is at stake and all that will happen is that either agents will breach the rules or players will dump their agents. Perhaps the latter is what The FA (as encouraged by The PFA) really wants. All of these restrictions are set out in Regulation H.

Having just written something cynical I immediately come to something which, in a vacuum, is commendable and very helpful to the honest agent; H6 provides on paper at least some protection for an agent from other predatory agents. An Authorised Agent can't directly or indirectly enter into a representation contract with a club or player where they have an exclusive agreement with you and other agents are also forbidden from even approaching your clients without your consent, save in the last month of his contract with you when it pretty much becomes open season. Other agents also can't 'induce' your player to break his contract with you. By 'induce' that not only means by persuasion but also by bribes, say in the shape of an expensive car or racehorse to your player or his mum or dad. Yes, trust me, there are no limits to what unscrupulous agents will do to land a big (or potentially big) client from whom they know they will earn far greater fees than the mere cost of an Audi or a thoroughbred.

Don't forget that you are also not supposed to be touting your players about without the permission of their current clubs. I have to confess that in the real world almost everybody does it and if you don't then you will soon lose your clients if they have expressed a desire to move on from their current clubs. However, there are ways and ways of doing it, although if at all possible it is clearly better and less illegal to discuss the position with the club. You do then run the risk of the club being able to claim that your client has effectively asked for a transfer and is therefore not entitled to the balance of any signing on fees. It's all a question of getting the right balance between operating within The FA Regulations, doing your best for your client and not getting a reputation within the industry whereby nobody trusts you further than they can throw you. Believe me, if you gave all the reputable agents a blank sheet of paper and a pen and asked them to write down the names of six agents with whom one should never deal then the same names would pop up in every list. I hasten to add that none of them are members of the recently formed Association of Football Agents (AFA) which, if I say so myself (and I am its secretary) is doing a sterling job in helping to improve the lot of agents big and small.

It pretty much goes without saying that if you are an agent then you shouldn't also be running a football club. Might just be the teensiest bit of conflict there. You will not be surprised to learn that The FA has gone even further and have said that you can not only not own more than 5% of a club but you also can't exercise any influence over any material, financial, commercial, administrative or managerial matters whether directly or indirectly. In an era when shadowy offshore figures do appear to 'own' players and to be able to use them to manipulate clubs (or at least make huge sums of money from transactions involving their own properties) I think this is not an unreasonable regulation. Let's hope that you actually get to the position when you have so much money you can choose between actually owning a club or continuing as an agent.

Control of a club or player here extends to any company over which you, in turn, also have control either directly or indirectly. The FA does insist upon full disclosure of all agreements that exist between agents and clubs whereby there can be payments but I think it unlikely that the sort of people at whom these regulations are aimed are going to be completely open in all their dealings and throw their books open to The FA.

When you are starting out it's likely that the best you can hope for is to sign up young players. The FA has sought to frustrate that approach as well as you now can't approach a player before he is 16. The problem here is that there are many agents out there who will be doing precisely that. They will be camping out on the doorsteps of the latest *wunderkinds'* parents' house and offering them all sorts of inducements to get little Johnny to sign for them. One of the parents will have to sign as guardian as well and that applies right up to the player's eighteenth birthday.

I'm sure it's not going to happen to you but if you are a naughty boy or girl then Big Brother in the shape of The FA has the right to suspend or withdraw your licence and if it manages to do that after you have exhausted all avenues of appeal then you will have to re-apply and there is no guarantee it will automatically be reissued.

This is a book about how to be a sports agent, not how to be a club, player or manager who has to comply with The FA Regulations but just take it as a given that they do and the clubs are responsible for the behaviour of their officials. So, if a manager wants to push one of your players to one of his favoured agents and bad-mouths you in the process then he is in breach of the rules and will be subject to a disciplinary procedure.

As I mentioned before, at first sight The FA Regulations, whilst imposing almost intolerable burdens, do also give some protection to the Authorised Agent. Clubs can only deal with the Authorised Agent, other clubs, or, and here is yet another sting in the tail, the player himself. I'll explain how that pans out when we look at representation agreements.

In a book this size I've not been able to give you too detailed an analysis of The FA Regulations and quite frankly had I done so then it would have been easy to justify a book on its own. But, hopefully I have been able to give you the flavour of just how difficult it is being made by The FA to carry on the business of a football agent in England nowadays. Even if you have a dispute with it you can't take it to court. Under the very sweeping Rule K all disputes between participants (and that includes The FA) have to go to arbitration and where The FA is responsible for convening the arbitration there is every possibility of it being the offending party (at least as far as you are concerned) whilst at the same time the judge and jury in relation to the decision concerning the dispute. Although, to be fair, most tribunal chairmen are fair-minded souls.

There have been problems in the past which needed addressing. There are many stories (some doubtless with more basis in truth than others) but one that you hear over and over again is that of a leading UK agent who knew a particular club (let's call them United) wanting a player (let's call him Bert) from another club (let's call them City). The first thing the agent did was to approach Bert and tell him that only he could get him a move to United and this persuaded Bert to dump his existing agent. The unscrupulous agent then toddled off to United and got them to retain him to procure the services of Bert and finally he went to City (who had by now given up all hope of keeping Bert) and asked for a commission from them for selling Bert. Not bad to be paid three times for the same transaction. Conflict? The agent had never heard of the word. How to make a lot of money very quickly? Yes. How to be a sports agent? I don't think so. But I truly believe that The FA has gone way over the top in regulating problems which were only being created by a small minority of agents. What has occurred has been a classic example of over-reaction leading to group punishment.

If you do break any of the regulations, what have you to fear? Well, you can be cautioned, censured, warned (do I hear you trembling in your boots?) or fined. That'll hurt when you have made a fortune from a deal! Your licence may be suspended and ultimately the licence can be withdrawn (in which case doubtless the disqualified agent will have someone waiting in the wings to step into his shoes). Certainly at least one agent who featured prominently in a 'bung' scandal seems to have had no great problem in carrying on in business for another decade.

If you are intending doing any business in the world of football then I do urge you to read The FA Regulations carefully. They are sure to make the winter evenings fly by.

How to Set Up a Sports Agency

I have explained how to set yourself up as a football agent but if you are going to be a genuine sports agent, you need to be able to deal with other disciplines. If you are thinking of representing anybody in a particular sport, all you need to do is telephone or write to the governing body before you do so and ask for details of their licensing regulations.

In this country, only athletics (and perhaps, to a lesser extent, boxing) makes it a precondition that you have to have knowledge of the sport. Yes, there is now the exam I have mentioned in football and also licensing regulations in rugby, but, as I have suggested, you won't have to be an Einstein to pass muster.

As with most things, the real exams to pass are those of the university of life. A jockey's agent would be unable to function if they didn't know the sport and those involved in it like the back of their hand. Boxing agents (and managers), often indistinguishable from promoters, have to know the real players in the sport as well as the nondescript journeymen who can be cannon fodder for their up-and-coming champions. If you want to represent cricketers you have to be able to spot the next Flintoff from the youngster who will be a squad player for Glamorgan (Wrexham and Glamorgan; I really have nothing against the Welsh, honest!) who will never produce enough income himself to enable you to make a living on the commission you may earn from him, or even to justify him paying you those commissions. This is where you have to be honest with yourself as well as your clients. It really is not difficult to sign clients. You can have a player roster of hundreds of wannabes in all kinds of sport. But ask yourself in each case, what can you do for them and do they really need you to do it? If a Football Conference club offers a player £250 per week that is probably all they can afford and you representing the player is not going to persuade them to pay him £1,000 per week. The net result will be him paying you your commission on his £250 per week and feeling bitter about it for the whole of the contract. Far better in PR terms is to give the player a little verbal guidance, monitor his career and if he does begin to develop gently remind him how you could have charged but chose not to (more of 'freebies' and 'loss leaders' later). Always keep in mind you are running a business, but all businesses also need regular promotion. It can be just as helpful to your business to have a young player singing your praises in the dressing room as to have your photo in the sports pages standing alongside an international as he signs for a Premier League club.

Not only do you need clients but you need an infrastructure. Working as a one-man band from a telephone box (or a mobile nowadays) with a Post Office box address does not inspire confidence in clients who are looking for some substance and stability in their representation. It may seem obvious but a pleasant office in which to greet your clients does help, as does a friendly voice to answer the telephone. So, although you don't need premises or a secretary (or Personal Assistants, as they like to be called nowadays), it does help. How much longer will it take before players become soccer operatives, I wonder?

It follows that some capital is required for the establishment of your new business. You need some money to pay the premiums for indemnity insurance and funds to pay for your rent (the odds are that a landlord will either want a rent deposit or a bank guarantee if you are just setting up in business). Equipment like a mobile phone, a fax, a computer and a blackberry aka crackberries (mine was called Bernie and I was so totally addicted to him that he had a breakdown and has been replaced by a sleek, silver model called Bernice) are necessities, not luxuries. Then you have to get stationery, a telephone, an Internet provider, broadband and regular publications relating to the sports in which you are to be involved. It all tots up. And the money doesn't come pouring in right away either, unless you are very lucky. It can be a little bit like being an estate agent – you can show a hundred people over a house over a period of six months but it is only when you finally sell it that you earn your commission. Most estate agents are marketing hundreds of houses to produce some cash flow. When you start out, the odds are that you'll have only a handful of clients – and you have to get those clients. Cash flow became significantly worse for football agents after the introduction of transfer windows. Deals can now only effectively be consummated during two periods a year, between the end of one season and the end of August in the next season and from post-Xmas through January. And as I have already mentioned, you don't even get all the money you earn in one hit nowadays because it is spread over the period of the contract. You may never get it if the player leaves the club before the expiry of the contract or if he enters into a new contract with the club after his agreement with you has ended without using your services. Although you might find a friendly bank that will 'factor' that for you, the interest you pay for that will reduce the income you finally receive in any event.

The fact of the matter is that getting the clients is hard, performing for them is difficult (they don't always seem to realise that they have to perform for you) and keeping them, even if you have performed, can be well nigh impossible. But let's start with getting them.

In today's market, the idea that you can just set up an office with all the attendant costs and wait for people to come in off the street like a private eye from a forties thriller is totally unrealistic. Even to consider setting up in the business you must have some connections, some links, some real hope of a foundation on which to build. It may be that you have played a sport, that you are related to or are friendly with a particular sportsperson, or that you are employing or going into partnership with somebody who has connections of their own. Any of these, or any combination of them, will do, but you also have to face the fact that sportspeople are starting their careers younger and younger and, if you don't get them young, the likelihood is that you will never get them at all.

The downside to representing young athletes is that it is highly unlikely that you will have any meaningful income during the period of your initial contract with them. There are always going to be exceptions, the footballers Wayne Rooney and Joe Cole and tennis star Andrew Murray for example, but even in football it is not unusual – and indeed it was becoming the norm – for parents of precocious teenagers (sometimes as young as ten or eleven) to have sought out or agreed to representation for them. As I mentioned in the previous chapter The FA regulations do put a stop to this, as you can't now sign a contract with a footballer who is under 16 even if his parents counter-sign as guardians. I am sure that participants will find creative ways to circumvent this. There is a world of difference between the parent who understands that their talented child needs to be looked after from an early age with a view to developing a relationship with their advisor and those who ruthlessly market their offspring to the highest bidder. It's not just in tennis that you meet the parents from hell.

So how does it work? First you spot a young talent, you speak to their dad (almost invariably the dad, though occasionally there can be mothers from hell as well). The dad may tell you how he would handle his son's career and then informs you that if you want to have the privilege of taking his place, then you need to pay him a certain sum of money (cash is not unheard of). Even if you agree to this outrageous demand, this may not be the end of the story because he may be dangling several lines in the water to compare the size of the fish he has caught, and you might find yourself tossed back in as small fry. Again, the FA regulations ban the payment of inducements to enter into contracts so I suspect we may be back to the days of passing over brown carrier bags at motorway service stations.

But think about it. If you are paying this premium to have the kid sign with you (I'll deal with minors signing contracts a bit later), you may well get the rough end of the deal. Their earning capacity as a schoolboy or scholarship player and even first-year professional (again, just looking at football, where this happens most often) is very limited. You work very hard to get them a bit of sponsorship in the shape of free kit and then have to prove yourself all over again when their contract comes up for renewal. Their profile is higher and bigger agencies are sniffing around, tempting them with all their connections and client rosters.

You have to bear in mind that a football agent's contract cannot be for a period of more than two years, nor can it be capable of being extended for more than two years. That means that you can't even have a clause stating that if you have made a certain amount of money for the client, you can automatically extend, a point I'll deal with in more detail when I analyse the contract between you and your client. There is, by the way, nothing to stop you getting the client to enter into two agreements, one for strict playing representation for the maximum two-year period and the other for a much longer period in respect of commercial representation. That commercial contract can be with a company and as I have said, you don't need to be licensed to negotiate commercial contracts. The FA, I am sure, will try to poke its nose into the terms of that commercial contract and will use the participating Authorised Agent as a weapon to enable it to satisfy its curiosity that nothing is going on between player and agent that could be construed as a breach of its precious rules. The reality of the situation is that if a player doesn't want to stay with you then you won't be able to make him. There are good legal and practical reasons for that, which I'll come to in good time. (I bet you are champing at the bit, trying to restrain yourself from flipping over pages like a mad thing.)

At the end of the day, you probably have no choice but to try to sign them as young as you can and hope for the best because the odds of getting an established player to sign for you once they are earning big money are long. (Yes, I know I said that kids tend to go elsewhere at the end of their first contract but it's Sod's law that they don't come to you!) And, it has to be said, most mums and dads of promising youngsters are really nice and only want the best for their offspring.

Don't be tempted to bankrupt yourself for the sake of getting in clients. You can offer all sorts of incentives; boots for which you pay yourself, free career-ending insurance, luxury gifts such as cars and holidays (although, as I say, no longer in the world of football). My view is that a player has to want to be represented by you, which means that you have to offer him your most valuable asset, yourself. Tell them that you will give 100% effort, honesty and integrity, not to mention total belief in their ability to succeed. All you ask in return is 100% loyalty and co-operation. It's a good deal and the sort of player who will not only accept it, but also keep to the bargain, is likely to prove the sort of player who will stick with you throughout his career.

You, in turn, have to be prepared to stick by them. Of course, you have signed them hoping they will play for Chelsea or Manchester United and England. Or Celtic or Rangers and Scotland. Or Cardiff and Wales (there I go again, I will be as popular in the Principality as Anne Robinson). But it may transpire that injury, ill-fortune or just loss of form sees them languishing in the lower regions of League Two. You have to stick by them. Not just because you should, but also because if you don't the player would be quite entitled to bad-mouth you amongst his peers as a fair-weather friend and ally. In this business performance counts for quite a lot, but reputation counts for more.

Recruiting Clients

This may come as a bit of a shock but, when you are starting out, clients don't come to you. There! Wasn't that revelation worth the purchase price of the book? The fact of the matter is that you should not really consider giving up the day job until such time as you have a nucleus of at least a dozen clients and have actually done a deal to get your cash flow going. You will be delighted to know that although you can't nick football clients from other agents that pursuant to Regulation H6 (c) of The FA Regulations you can 'publicise your services generally'. So, that's alright then.

Many wannabe agents do find work with an already established agency before launching out on their own. If you are one of them, then check your contract of employment carefully. It will almost certainly contain restrictive covenants. At the very least these will stop you approaching existing clients of your employer (not unreasonable if you think about it and once you are up and running yourself you wouldn't like it to be done to you... Do unto others as you would have done unto yourself... Not a bad maxim for a generally difficult business). The restrictions may go further. They may restrain you from talking to potential clients with whom your employer-agency is in discussions; they may stop you setting up an office within a certain radius from their office; they may even stop you operating as a sports agent for a period of time, full stop. The FA Regulations do provide that if you work for a company and the representation contract is with you personally then, if you leave the player has some choices to make. Your departure effectively brings the contract to an end so the player can either stay with the agency and re-sign with another Authorised Agent, or leave the agency altogether, or sign with you personally. This last course depends upon the strength of your restrictive covenant with the agency. That, of course, cuts both ways depending upon the stage of your career. If you are working for somebody you want them to be as weak as possible, but if you have become successful and are running your own business then you want them to be drawn so tightly that your ex-employee can't breathe let alone steal your clients.

All of this ignores one rather vital point, namely that it is impossible to make a client agree to have you represent him. It has always been the case in English law that a contract for personal services (no, I don't mean that kind of personal services) is not enforceable by way of injunction as the courts believe there is an adequate remedy in damages. Consequently, against the background of The FA Regulations (inequitable as they are in this instance) it is better to pre-empt the situation and actually to insert a clause in the employment contract allowing the employee after he leaves to act for players he has signed, provided he still accounts to you for what you would have earned whilst he was with you for the duration of the contract with the player. And maybe you can also negotiate a smaller slice of the cake for ongoing contracts. Much better to bite the bullet than to have to go to court to test the enforceability of the restrictive covenants.

Depending on how they are drawn, and also dependent upon how draconian they are, then they may not even be enforceable. You can try to go too far and find that you have not even left home base. This may be a moment to take advice from your friendly neighbourhood lawyer (I was going to say solicitor, but I recall that has a different meaning in the States. I always remember on my first visit seeing a sign on the front door of a house, saying NO SOLICITORS. Very nice, I thought, but basically it means no door-to-door hawkers.) Mind you know some lawyers who might have been better equipped life of door-to-door selling of *Encyclopaedia Britannica* th ...n arguing their unfortunate clients' cases in court.

However, let's assume that you are free to trade and can, within reason, approach whomsoever you like. The odds are that most of the clients you would most like to represent already have an established relationship with a representative. Don't be dismayed. Whilst there are quite strict rules in football, pursuant to the agents' regulations, forbidding you from enticing a player away from a valid contract, there is, in my view, nothing wrong in introducing yourself to a player and if he tells you he already has an agent then two questions are permissible. One is to enquire if he is happy with his representation, and the other is to ask when his agreement with his current agent expires. Just giving him your card and asking him to contact you when he is out of contract, is not, I believe, a breach of the rules. I know The FA Regulations say you can only approach a player in the last month of his representation agreement with his existing agent, but how do you know unless you ask the two questions I have suggested? Maybe you want to comply with The FA Regulations to the letter and just ask the one question, namely when does his contract with his agent expire? The FA are hoping to keep a full register of representation contracts but whether Data Protection allows that to be freely accessible I am not sure, nor whether it is a good thing to have other agents keeping a watching brief on your contract with your player as the clock runs down. However, if you go further than that preliminary enquiry, then not only may you put your licence at risk, but you may also find yourself at the wrong end of a writ claiming that you have procured a breach of contract. Always remember that, in football at least, the natural life of a contract can only be two years and however well a representative may have done in those two years, he is still up for review at the end of that time. Sorry to keep repeating that but it is vital to know that there is no real security of tenure in football at least.

The fact of the matter is that recruiting players is very hard. When I first began it was astonishingly simple. I recruited Chris Waddle and Paul Gascoigne as clients simply by going up to Newcastle, knowing somebody at the club, and being a Newcastle United supporter. I got Alan Shearer as a client by writing to him, answering a letter he sent me (drafted for him by his old mentor) with a lot of questions and then going to see him at his home. Then it got a bit more tricky and I actually employed guys to help me recruit. They would make a cold call, or simply leave a message at the club and following on to that it was a question of meeting up for a cup of tea (you would be amazed as to how few footballers drink coffee) in a local hotel, explaining what I was about and then giving them the contract to consider. I never ever asked a potential client to sign on the spot. For starters I always advised them to get independent advice on my form of contract and I was always full of admiration for those who would take it to a lawyer and ask for a few amendments. I also think that most sportspeople don't like to feel railroaded or pressurised into signing anything. However, nowadays, you have to balance that by the fact that there is such extraordinary competition to sign clients and I must say that my current experience is that if a player doesn't sign quickly then he doesn't sign at all. However, The FA does now require the player to be advised to take independent legal advice and to sign off to say they have declined that opportunity. Mind you, there is advice and there is advice and many lawyers, however competent in their own fields, just don't understand the dynamics of football. There is much to be said for following the example of the music industry where managers pay specialist music lawyers a fairly modest fee to advice the musician or band before they enter into the contract.

It does take some experience to recognise the time-wasters in terms of potential clients and those who are even more devious and like to keep several agents hanging on to see what they can get out of each of them before signing. Quite often that kind of character doesn't sign at all, or goes off and signs with another totally different agent. Always be wary of players who ask for boots or kit before they commit themselves. It doesn't augur well.

To be a successful sports agent you do need to know a fair bit about sport and like it well enough to be prepared to spend a large amount of time watching it. Personally, I have steered away from recruitment at matches and have preferred to arrange meetings in the more relaxed environment of a restaurant, hotel or home. But the fact remains that if you go to any match, however obscure the contestants, you will find a plethora of agents waiting like vultures to swoop on potential warm flesh the minute their target leaves the showers. Indeed, it has not been unknown for an agent to button-hole a player as he makes his way off the pitch, muddy and sweaty, on his way to the dressing room. I wouldn't pour cold water on the idea of attending matches. Some players really do want you to see them play on a regular basis, though I always felt that had no effect on my ability to represent them more than adequately. As long as you know the parameters of the financial packages being paid at the club with which you are negotiating, why should it make you a better negotiator just because you happened to see the club's last three matches? But try telling that to a sportsman when you are recruiting him and it will not get the greatest reception. I certainly lost at least one client because I didn't go to watch him play at Brighton and his 'new' agent did. I would have liked to have been a fly on the wall to have heard the touchline chat-up lines.

It is interesting that rugby and cricket agencies are dominated by ex-rugby players and ex-cricketers. I hate rugby, yet still have had several rugby clients, each of whom have vied in the past to be the one to get me to see my first live rugby match. When England won the World Cup I managed to avoid watching even the adverts at half-time. So when the Victory Parade occurred in London's Regent Street right by my office I was more than a little peeved not to be allowed to re-cross the road back to my office with my cup of recently purchased soup.

'Don't you want to watch the parade?' a puzzled policeman asked.

'What sort of World Cup is it when you don't have to qualify to get there, that when you get there you have to play Western Samoa, and when you win the fans behave impeccably?'

The copper looked at me in despair and ushered me personally across the road.

Now, I really don't recommend that approach to the fledgling agent. I also don't recommend dishonesty. So, to kick off, before you attain my gravitas that allows me to get away with being a crotchety old man, you should focus on the sports that you really like. In any event, assuming that you are going to try and aim for young, emerging players, you won't actually even know about them unless you are an aficionado of the sport. With young players, attendances at reserve team fixtures (usually in the afternoons, anyway) or youth team matches *are* helpful and can be a selling feature in your pitch to the player.

Nothing beats personal contacts. If you are given a phone number of a potential client by his girlfriend's brother, or a neighbour, or his dad's workmate, then you have a much better chance of getting to first base. First base used to be a meeting at which I would hand over the proposed contract, now it is a telephone conversation which may or may not result in a meeting. Players may not necessarily have had the best of educations but it does not take them long to become streetwise and recognise that they are a commodity in a seller's market... oh, and by the way, they are also the seller!

The one thing I am trying to bang home to you, is that if you are going to set up a sports agency don't go to all the effort and expense in the hope and prayer that you just might get a client or two. That goes beyond the brave, beyond foolhardy and borders on the fringes of financial suicide. Assuming you do have a couple of clients and a few leads, as I said before, wait until you have built the business up into real potential before burning your boats and going full-time. Unless you have a very generous parent, backer or partner prepared to fund you throughout what could be a very difficult and rather expensive first couple of years of trading.

If you are going to a bank for funding then they will want a business plan and this is just about the hardest business in the world for which to write one. You just don't know from day to day what is going to come in. You can be sitting there, head in hands, with a loaded revolver on the desk before you. There is one day to go before the transfer window closes and suddenly you get a call from a Premiership club. The player they have been chasing for weeks has just signed for a rival. They are interested in one of your strikers. You have to get him (and yourself) to the club, him for his medical, you to negotiate terms. You make the calculations in your head. You are saved for another six months. You put the revolver back in the drawer and head for the car. That may be a bit of an exaggeration, but it really is like that. Every close season I would review my players, wonder who would be moving, establish some targets. And every year something would come at the death out of the blue.

So, back to the business plan. Quite frankly, you just have to play the percentage game. You have 20 players. Let us say five of them will move clubs and three will have new contracts offered by their clubs based on the unexpired term of their existing contract. An average value of the new contracts will be half a million pounds over their term. 5% means 25k a contract divided by an average of a four-year term so that is £6,250 pa per player, times 8 and you are predicting a turnover of 50k a year. It really is 'how long is a piece of string?' The situation has become increasingly worse in terms of cash flow as first of all clubs when they were allowed to pay the fees spread them over the term of the contract and now you have to face up to the problem of prising money out of your clients. I have been very fortunate during my career as with one or two notable exceptions my clients have been very happy to pay for my services. But, the fact is that the players I have represented and continue to represent are not the norm. Most players don't like paying and even if they start to pay you what is due to you there is no way you will be able to bank on receiving all the payments. Somewhere along the line they will negotiate you down either off their own back or encouraged by a rival agent and sadly there is nothing in The FA Regulations which gives you any protection or pursuant to which it will assist you in making recovery of what is properly due. Another opportunity missed and another chance for The PFA to gather in discontented players. And what is aggravating is that they are not discontented because of anything bad you have done but merely because they have to pay for it.

If, as I've mentioned, you are dealing with very young sportsmen and women then you are also going to be dealing with parents. Every sport has its fair share of parents from hell, but generally speaking you will find that they only want the best for their children and it is up to you to convince them that you are the best. Here, I have the advantage, because the odds are that I am older than my readers. There are days when I feel older than anybody who can still read without the aid of a magnifying glass. Parents can be reluctant to entrust the future of their offspring to somebody who could very well be their offspring himself. But, you still have to try and convince them. So what do you have to sell?

Well, youth and enthusiasm for one (or two, actually). Plus you have energy, commitment and everything to prove. You don't have so many clients so every client isn't a major one as far as you are concerned and that is where you can score over the larger agencies. I've given you the patter about honesty and loyalty ratio and I don't think I need to tell you the percentages of who keeps which side of the bargain more often. With some rare exceptions, and in that case I have been very fortunate to have some remarkably loyal clients who have stuck by me through thick and thin and whose careers have spiralled with all the temptations that entails; you are only as good as your last deal. Sportsmen have very short memories and gratitude is not a natural emotion for them. But that's alright, too. You can get too close to your clients as well and sometimes it is best to keep the relationship strictly professional. There are grave dangers in going out on the town with your clients. If he turns up for training the next day with a gigantic hangover, or worse still, turns up on the front pages of the tabloids for some night club exploit, and you were with him, then that could mean your entire reputation going down the tubes. At the very least you will become *persona non grata* at that particular club and, apart from the goodwill of your clients, the goodwill of clubs comes very high on the agenda. Players need you to have a good line of communication with their employers and it can become very difficult if you cannot get a meeting with the manager or chairman swiftly, when the need arises. Of course, you have to be mindful of conflict. Clubs will try and get you onside thinking they can do a soft deal with you because they have tossed a few crumbs of business your way. It is a very narrow path to tread and the correct route only comes with experience.

You have to be prepared to learn from your mistakes. Something you have said to a parent lost you a potential client, so you are careful not to say the same thing again. And whilst we are back on the subject of parents you have to be aware that even the nice parents have an inflated view of Little Johnny's ability. They will have watched from the touchline as he stood head and shoulders above his contemporaries at school and youth club level. They will firmly believe that qualifies him to play for Chelsea, Manchester United, Arsenal or Liverpool. I have had fathers who have ruined their sons' careers because they had unrealistic opinions as to their kids' abilities. Unfortunately, those opinions rub off on the lad himself and managers are quick to spot individuals who have unjustified big heads. One father actually phoned a club with whom I had negotiated for his son and told the Chairman that he didn't think his son was going to be paid enough. I knew that for all the player's inexperience I had got him a deal that put him in the top 10% of earners at the club. The Chairman told him that if that was the case the offer was withdrawn and he could look elsewhere. The father then had the nerve to come back to me and ask if I would split my commission with him on future deals! The player ended up with his career in ruins and playing abroad in a very minor footballing country. You have to remember that football is a village and that word spreads like wildfire amongst its inhabitants. Everybody likes gossip and if one of your players, or you, yourself, gain a reputation for being difficult, that will take a very long time to shake off and may be something with which you will have to live forever. Fathers (and sometimes mothers) either think they can do better than you or else think it immoral that you should earn anything from their offspring. Hence their desire to try to get you to pay them for the privilege of representing their child. In football The FA Regulations say that 'Close Relations' can act for the player but can't charge. It seems to me therefore that you won't be able legally to share your fees with a parent because under The FA Regulations you have to disclose the details of everybody you are paying out of the deal. There is no doubt in my mind that the practice of parents seeking rewards either in advance or from fees earned will continue and you have to decide whether or not you want to join in what I consider to be a highly immoral game. If the parents really cared about their kids then they would just want the best person to be acting for them and to be fair some of them do just that. But some of them don't. Some of them see their kids as a meal ticket for life, an excuse never to have to work again and they are the ones of whom you should be most careful. Never put yourself in a position where anybody has a hold over you and can effectively 'blackmail' you into doing things that can get you into deep trouble. It's just so much better to be able to put your head on the pillow at night and go to sleep without worrying about whether or not there is going to be a dawn raid on your home by HM Customs and Excise or several large gentlemen dressed in blue carrying search warrants.

So back to honesty. You do need to be honest, but brutal honesty is not necessarily the best way to recruit clients. Sometimes, you just have to listen and hope that it will become apparent even to the parent wearing the largest pair of rose-tinted spectacles that their son who can't make it into the Mansfield first team is unlikely ever to grace the pitch at

Stamford Bridge. Unless, that is, he decided to take up an alternative career as a groundsman. At the start of a player's career, just as is the case at the start of your relationship with the player, everything is possible. It may not be probable, but it is possible. So the best response to an overly optimistic parent is 'We'll see. All I can promise is that if he does it on the pitch then I'll do it off the pitch for him'.

That's the one thing over which we, as sports agents, have little control. We can't kick or hit the ball for them, we can't stop it flying into the net, we can't get a hole in one, or make a solo run for a touchdown, or land a KO punch in the first round, or serve any number of aces to win set after set. All we can do is to maximise the income of those who do have that touch of genius to attain those heights, and once the client is yours to do everything possible to keep him happy. Sports agency is a little like juggling. You just can't afford to take your eye off any of the balls

The Agency Contract

Let us try and examine the document you get them to sign and yet again let's deal with football first. Unless you are a lawyer just providing exempt services you are now going to have to get your players to enter into an agreement with you in an FA-approved form and have that agreement registered with The FA.

That agreement can provide for all sorts of different ways of payment as long as the payment comes from the player including, if you are a lawyer, an hourly rate. Indeed, even if you are a Licensed Agent you can charge an hourly rate. In reality, you will find you won't even be able to charge yourself out at a full rate because there has to be a bit of speculative work. Can you imagine flying up to Newcastle, sitting down all day with a great young prospective athlete and then sending them a bill for 8 hours' work (excluding travelling time) at £450 plus VAT per hour? It follows that if anybody out there is thinking of starting a sports law department including athlete representation, then they'll need some very supportive and understanding partners.

As far as the representation contract is concerned, it is worth noting that both The FA and FIFA Regulations have annexed to them a suggested form of contract, although it won't surprise you to learn that the document is not awfully attractive in terms of protecting the agent. Perhaps, rather than setting exams, FA and FIFA representatives should be sitting them. (I can recommend a very good postgraduate Sports Law examination course at King's College London, which coincidentally I helped establish and for which I still provide part of the lectures.)

The standard representative's agreement in football provided by FIFA is skeletal and minimal to say the least – parties, duration, remuneration, exclusivity (or not as the case may be), applicable law and that's it. But, although you have to use The FA precedent form's compulsory terms as a template under the new FA Regulations, let's see what a real agreement should contain and why.

Now I am not beating the drum for solicitors, but I would strongly recommend that you get your standard agreement drafted by a lawyer. And not just any lawyer. You wouldn't go to a divorce specialist to buy your house, or a music lawyer to buy a ship (well, you might, but in each case it would be a big mistake). No, you do need to go to a lawyer who has experience in the field of sport, no pun intended, but as it's there and it's not bad, I might as well leave it in. If you invest some money in the drafting, or at the very least the checking, of a contract, then you do have some security. If a client reneges and you sue and he (or she) manages to wriggle free from the representative agreement because it is defective then you will be able to sue the lawyer for negligence, and have the comfort of knowing that he has some insurance to rely upon. That claim can be quite substantial. If the client is young and established then you could be looking at a loss of several hundreds of thousands of pounds over the period of the contract from which he has escaped. I have limited this chapter to the representation of individuals but you may, of course, find yourself representing a club in relation to procuring a player (again there is a precedent in The FA Regulations) or with a view to arranging matches for them (don't forget this needs a different kind of FIFA licence).

As to the contents of a representation agreement, I make no apology for the fact that I am using football (soccer) as a template. There are several clauses which are particular to that sport, but generally speaking what goes for football goes for most other sports as well. You are not tied down to a two-year contract without automatic renewal (or indeed any option to renew) when it comes to the majority of sports, but that peculiarity makes little difference to the body of the agreement.

Obviously FIFA and The FA are right about parties – but that is not very difficult. There will be the player and the agent or if the player is a minor (under 18) then it will be their guardian as well. Although astonishingly, and I believe wrongly, The FA does not want the guardian to be a party to the agreement lodged with them and have suggested this be contained in a separate document. Go figure? I think they may feel that whilst the Authorised Agent and the player are participants the player's guardian is not. In any event, there is always the chance that a minor can get out of a contract signed by their guardian upon attaining their majority if the contract is too onerous, which is why you have to be especially careful in the drafting when dealing with young athletes. You must set out clearly the terms of reference. Sometimes you may be the exclusive agent for all purposes. Sometimes it will be non-exclusive for some and exclusive for others or non-exclusive all round. Alternatively, you may have no authority in some areas at all.

A good example would be the world of cricket. Cricket-playing contracts are fairly standard and many cricketers realise there is little chance of beefing up something that is offered to them by their county on a take-it-or-leave-it basis. Central contracts which are offered to the core Test players (that's internationals for our Transatlantic cousins) are what they are as the retainer payments are paid from central funding and there is a standard form of contract. There are of course exceptions such as big names from abroad who come over to play for a county as their permitted overseas player. However, you can represent a player for their commercial contracts but not for their playing deal and certainly with English cricket occasionally riding the crest of a wave there can be more money in representing some of our leading personality Test players than minor Premier League footballers. By the by, that's as good a reason as any for not ignoring some of our so-called minority sports. With England's rugby players winning one World Cup and getting to the final of another, our cricketers winning the Ashes in my lifetime. Lewis Hamilton likely to be a major motor racing star for many years to come, boxers like Hatton and Calzaghe becoming world wide celebrities, who is to say that other sports won't throw up unsuspected heroes if Gold medals are won at the 2012 Olympics on our home patch? Of course, you can't make a living just by representing hockey players or 3-Day Eventers but that is not to say you shouldn't consider representing them either. At the very least they may be able to get you tickets for the Olympics. Me, I'm looking at recruiting beach volleyball players.

If it is to be exclusive then good catch-all wording would be representation in connection with 'the development, negotiation and organisation of all income-producing activities which are or may become available to the Player/ Athlete/Sportsperson (as the case may be) in any part of the world arising from the Player's career as an athlete. and from their name, image, nickname and reputation'. Again, bear in mind that if you are dealing with a sport that limits the playing contract representation to a period of time then you may well want to have a separate agreement in respect of the commercial marketing of the image. There, at least you can have representation by a company rather than a licensed individual. You should also consider the possibilities of your client having a non-resident company set up to deal with his commercial interests. This only works if your client is a foreign, non-domiciled individual and should be set up before he comes to ply his trade in the United Kingdom. Just a note of caution here, our good friends at the Inland Revenue are having a good hard look at anything that can be construed as an 'offshore' arrangement so you need to be satisfied that there are genuine grounds for establishing such an entity. Once more, it may be worthwhile investing a bit of money for some tax advice. The same will apply when I come to playing contracts for foreign players and the question of removing image rights there as well and working with the club to set up an offshore tax saving arrangement. This is not intended to be a legal text book, but do bear in mind the difference between tax avoidance (legal) and tax evasion (illegal). As the author of another erudite tome entitled 'How to Complain' I don't want to be receiving complaint letters on HM Prison notepaper.

There has to be a bit of legalese about the contract but, on the other hand, it also has to be clear and simple. You are a professional (possibly) and you are dealing with someone who left school at 16 without qualifications (probably) and if disputes arise later, you can be quite sure that any court will bend over backwards to try and help the uneducated youngster. I have made specific reference to 'name, image and nickname' because even without the physical presence of the athlete they can be valuable. There is no time here to go into intellectual property protection in depth (that's what they are, by the way – the name, image and nickname – intellectual property or IP among the experts, or clever houses in my wife's little joke) but for heaven's sake go to a lawyer or an intellectual property specialist (like a Trade Mark Agent... I mention that just to show I'm not always beating up work for lawyers) and get whatever you have or might have protected by registration. Protection, even of a signature, can be valuable in the long run and if you are acting for a big name or a potentially big name, it's even worthwhile creating a caricature. You can then put that on a product label (à la Disney) and show that what is being sold is authorised merchandise. It takes longer to be able to protect an actual name but it is far easier to achieve that end now than it was when I first set out in this business. Certainly the likes of Alan Shearer, Wayne Rooney and even Sir Alex Ferguson have been able to register just their own name without any logo, signature or caricature.

The term or period of the management contract is important. Clearly you would like to tie up your client for as long as possible but you have to be mindful of a court deciding that the contract is unfair and therefore void or voidable, i.e. invalid from the start or so badly drafted that a half-decent lawyer can get your client out of it. As already mentioned, football representation contracts can only be for a two-year maximum and cannot contain a clause for automatic renewal. Even an option to renew dependent upon the amount of money actually made for the footballer isn't binding because the contract cannot be capable of running for more than two years. However, what can be fair and reasonable in non-football contracts is to insert a clause giving you the sort of right to automatic renewal in the case of such success. It is not unusual in the music business for a manager to have an option to extend if they get their client a record deal or for the client to be able to terminate if there is any period of, say, nine months, when the client-artist doesn't have a recording contract.

So, in sports terms, if you procure your client valuable endorsements or sponsorship contracts that prove you have performed, you could put in a clause that says that, provided you get your client endorsements up to a certain reasonable value, you get the right to take up your option. And you can counterbalance that by saying that if during any, say, 12-month period the endorsement/sponsorship income falls below an agreed minimum then the client can terminate. So, no pressure there then.

Make sure for your own protection that it is the getting of the endorsement/sponsorship deal that triggers off the option and not the receipt of the monies. The actual monies can take a fair time to come through and it would be grossly unfair for you to do a deal for a client and then let another representative get the benefit of it just because you have allowed your contract to slip away through a loophole. What you should also not forget is a clause to say that you will also receive commission on any endorsement contract that survives the termination of your representation and any renewal of any contract introduced and negotiated by you, whether or not your representation of the player has ceased. Why should his new agent rake in the 20%'s on deals into which he has had no input? There is a middle road here if your successor has upped the ante on a deal through his negotiating skills, but even there you should seek some kind of run-off commission, maybe reducing by 5% per annum for the next four years.

It may seem a bit pedantic, but you should get your client to warrant that, a) they have no other representative at the time they sign your contract and, b) they agree not to appoint anybody else during the period of the contract or any extension of it. Believe me, it happens. Sportsmen are notorious for yielding to pressure and quite frequently will sign a document just to get rid of a persistent suitor. I have experienced several instances when an agent has virtually camped outside the front door of a prospective client. These people have missed their vocations. They would have made fortunes selling double-glazing. Mind you, exclusivity in football is not a lot of help when The FA specifically allows a player to represent himself.

Sportsmen are also notorious for sticking their heads in the sand and hoping that the fact they have signed with two, or sometimes even more, agents, will not cause them a problem and that everybody involved (except themselves) will have a fight and then sort it out. That is something else you will have to get used to if you are to succeed as a sports agent. Sportsfolk may be the bravest in their chosen field but are incredible cowards off it. I know (as do many of my contemporaries) that unanswered and unreturned calls usually signify bad news. If that happens then the odds are that there will shortly follow either a letter purporting to terminate your representation or a phone call from a mum, dad or even wife to ask you to stop calling because it is upsetting Little Johnny who doesn't want you to act for him any more even though you made him a million quid last season. There are quite a few examples of problems with ungrateful clients. A typical case is when you find a player a club, he makes the excuse that it is too far to travel, or that he needs to think about it, and suddenly you see on teletext that he has signed for another club. He may have done the deal himself, he may have used another agent, but the fact remains that you will have done a barrowload of work and now will be chasing your fees (now not allowed in football under the FA Agents' Regulations). You can contact the club and persuade them to pay, you can try and call your erstwhile player (odds on he'll have changed his mobile number within a matter of days) but at the end you have to make a judgement call as to whether or not you will pursue your claim through the courts. And if you do, you will become the villain of the piece, bad-mouthed throughout the dressing room as an agent who sues his clients. My advice though is that it is better to let the footballing world know that you mean business rather then being regarded as a soft touch. That whole scenario is another reason why your contract with your clients has to be water-tight. Oh, and by the way, it's not a bad idea to get the lawyer who drafted it to be responsible for pursuing bad debts that arise under it. No pressure there either. The situation has been assisted in football by The FA insisting that all representation contracts are registered with them. However, in law, if the contract is enforceable, the fact you have not registered does not necessarily mean it can't be enforced through the courts. So there could be the scenario whereby you get a footballer to sign, you register but he doesn't tell you that he has already signed a contract with another agent which although not registered pre-dates your own. The FA will only recognise your contract but will the courts apply the same test? The answer is I don't know and we will have to wait for the first case of that nature before the answer becomes clear. Typical lawyer's explanation wasn't it?

The whole question of exclusivity is, under the new FA Agents Regulations an enormous problem. Players are permitted to represent themselves. So, what is the point of the agreement, I hear you ask. I can't tell you, I answer. The FA seem to have a blind spot on the issue. Their answer is that you can insert a clause providing that the player has to pay your contractual fee even if he excludes you from the deal and negotiates for himself. This is small comfort. In the first place you would probably have got him a better deal and thus earned more money, secondly it does not do your reputation in the business any good if your players are forever running off and doing their own deals leaving you to pursue them for fees and thirdly, what guarantee do you have that you will even know when a contract has been concluded between the club and the player? If he doesn't tell you, then you are left to rely upon the newspapers and club websites for information.

The possibility of falling out with a client and the need to create a paper trail if that were to happen makes the need for a constant stream of information to the client vital. Information as far as the client is concerned is everything. Clients, in whatever sport, like to know what is going on and, indeed, like to be assured that something is going on even if it's not producing any results. Whatever may happen, always be sure to call your clients at least once every couple of weeks even if it is just a matter of seeing how they are, asking after the family, making sure they are well supplied with kit etc. And whenever you do that, make an attendance note and keep it on his file. You never know when it may become useful. I wish I had a hundred pounds for every time I have heard a sportsperson moan that he never heard from his agent. I've been on the receiving end and a quick note back setting out the innumerable calls that have been made, together with supporting documentation, does wonders to jog the memory. As I've said on many occasions the one thing about which you won't be disappointed in the sports industry is that you'll be disappointed. Think about it. It does make sense.

Similarly, it gives the client comfort if there is a clause in the management agreement which says that you won't open negotiations with any third parties without the client's prior knowledge and consent. This works both ways. You may feel you would like to surprise your client with the news that you have got them a great deal but you will be the one who ends up with egg on your face if your client doesn't want to do the deal. You lose credibility both with your client and the sponsor or club you have dealt with who will have been assured by you that you have the authority to conclude a deal for your client.

You may have an even more serious problem on your hands if you have committed your client to a deal without telling them. I have not known a club argue that a player is committed just because his agent says he is, but it is an interesting scenario. They are pursuing two players. You negotiate a deal for your client, agree all the terms and confirm the time your client will attend to sign. They withdraw from their other negotiations on the back of that and the other player joins another suitor. Your client then changes his mind and says he is not coming. Might the club not have an action against you for damages, if not against your client as well? No court in the world would make your client sign for the club if he didn't want to, but I can see instances where courts might be only too happy to imply a contract where the club has been dealing with an agent with implied authority to conclude the deal.

There may be even greater exposure in relation to commercial deals. The company with which you have negotiated may well have assumed you had authority to commit your client and consider there to be a binding contract. They may well have acted upon it by putting together a preliminary business plan or even designing and printing up marketing material. If you then can't get your boy (or girl) to fulfil the terms of the deal, then the company may end up suing you for breach of contract and, as I say, if they have already laid out some money to set up the promotion or lost the opportunity of getting someone else because they thought they had your client, then the damages claim can be quite substantial.

Even once you have opened negotiations, then you should contract to keep your client fully informed of all developments in relation to such negotiations.

Never, ever contract to use best endeavours to do anything. (Although I have to say that the standard wording in the compulsory form annexed to the new FA Agents Regulations does use the words 'best endeavours'. I have yet to discover if this is one of the clauses that can be watered down by your own additional clauses. For the sake of this section let's assume it does or if it doesn't, then what I have to say would, in any event, apply in other sports.

It is very easy to lean over backwards to please and to try and get a sportsperson to sign with you, but don't go overboard. Promises made to persuade someone to sign with you and which are later broken are almost always remembered. The only promises you can make are to be honest and do your best. So if that is the case, do I hear you ask, why not agree to provide your best endeavours?

The answer, as you may have guessed, lies not in the soil but in the law. 'Best endeavours' can be interpreted in an almost draconian way. A footballing goalkeeper that you represent could argue that you are in breach as soon as you sign up a second keeper. How can you provide them with a 'best endeavours' service if you are also acting for a rival? It's the same story if you act for two boxers fighting at the same weight. Or two tennis players of roughly the same ability. Which one of them do you put forward for the best bout or wild card entry into tournaments when you can bet your bottom dollar they will each believe they are the better of the two? So just stick to 'reasonable' endeavours and it is a reasonable commitment then that can be interpreted by the parties – or ultimately by a court – in a reasonable manner.

In that way, agree to promote your client's career and try and get them income-producing activities (don't forget you have an incentive because you are getting a slice of those activities) but never guarantee you will get them. At the risk of being boring (I know... I know) you can only do what is reasonably possible to try to get the deals. And if you do get them and you follow the steps set out in the contract (prior consent, information, authority), then get your client to agree to enter into the sponsorship or playing contract – and not just enter into it but carry out its obligations to the best of their ability (here it is not unreasonable to use the word 'best' because if someone is paying your bloke a six-figure sum to promote their product, you can be pretty sure they'll want value for money).

What I have done to help you in respect of footballers is to annex not only The FA draft form of contract but also a form that I drafted and which The FA have approved. That form is being used by several agencies now and in a perfect world we would like to have a standard form of representation agreement being used by all members of The Association of Football Agents. Sadly, it's not a perfect world any more than it's a level playing field.

Representing a Club

The FA Regulations also provide a standard form of Representation Contract between Agent and Club, obviously only as far as football is concerned. This can either be exclusive or non-exclusive, but again can't be for more than two years. It can be renewed but not for more than two years at a time.

Absurdly the club is not obliged to use the agent's services and can act for itself even if the agreement is exclusive. Makes no sense to me or anybody else on the agency side of the game. It's for you to insert a clause to say that if they choose to do that then they still have to pay you.

Be careful because if the agreement is non-exclusive and if it is deemed that you haven't performed any of the services referred to in the contract then you get paid nothing. It may be a matter of dispute as to who has actually found a buyer for a player on behalf of a club so be sure to create a paper trail.

The fee has to be set out clearly as do the terms upon which it is to be paid, but it is only payable when you submit your invoice. If you don't want to go broke then make sure your accounting system is efficient.

Payment is conditional on the player in question becoming a registered player for the club and REMAINING SO ON THE DUE DATES. So, if he leaves your payments end.

You have to pay your own expenses unless otherwise agreed so don't go bombing off to clubs abroad thinking the club is obliged to pick up the tab. They are not unless there is a clause to that effect.

You have to give certain warranties. Odd wording here. You must provide the services to the BEST of you're ability but are only obliged to use REASONABLE ENDEAVOURS in connection therewith. Go figure! Again!

You have to keep the club in the loop at all times and not negotiate with any third parties without their consent. That means if you find a buying club that the club doesn't like you may well have wasted your time, so probably best to get a list of clubs with whom they will deal in relation to the player as early as possible. Still, possible for you to introduce a buyer and then for the club to circumvent you as set out above,

Obviously you have to hold a licence at all times so if you retire with payments still due to you then you may not get them. You also have to be insured at all times. You can't be paid by the player, nor can you share your fee with the player, a club or pay it to any third party who may assist in doing that. Also goes without saying you can't give a 'kick-back' to anybody at the club.

You give nine warranties. The club gives you two back in return. Life just ain't fair to agents. All the club agrees to do is to comply with The FA Regulations and provide you with the information you need to perform the services in the contract. Big deal!

The contract comes to an end if you lose your licence or it is suspended but only when you have exhausted the appeal processes. It can also be terminated for cause which is normal. If it is terminated then that's the end of your payments as well.

There are some extraordinary provisions if you work for an 'Organisation'. If you leave then the club can either continue to be represented by you (subject to any restrictive covenants you may have with your former employer) terminate and enter into another agreement with another Authorised Agent at the Organisation or just terminate without any other obligations than to pay any sums due. So, basically what that means is that the Organisation, which is not a 'participant' or in any way subject to The FA Regulations can lose substantial sums of money just because one of their employees takes it into his head to leave. Even if they have restrictions on him that won't mean that the club can't call it a day and avoid any further payments. You really couldn't make this sort of cloud cuckoo land stuff up, could you?

You have to keep the terms of the contract confidential so forget the kiss-and-tell autobiography and you can't assign or sub-contract without the club's consent. That's really going to help the transaction move on apace.

You can't enter into any side contracts that don't comply with The FA Regulations and anything that's not in the main contract still has to be registered with The FA. Big Brother wants to know everything that occurs in his Fiefdom.

If there is a dispute you can't even take the club to court because you have to arbitrate under Rule K. And be very careful because the arbitrator can insist upon you putting up a large amount of security for the costs before you even get to a hearing, something you would probably not have to do if you issued proceedings through the courts.

So, all that is great fun and games and I am sure that having taken all of that on board you are going to focus on representing players rather than clubs. But, and it's a big but, it is much easier to be paid by the club. They actually have the money and I am sure that unscrupulous agents are still going to avoid entering into contracts with their players just so that they can act for a club when the player makes his move. If The FA finds out then it will be a disciplinary matter but the financial rewards may be so great that some (or maybe many) agents will still take their chances. If The FA had not made The Regulations so draconian when it came to getting paid by anybody other than the player, if you act for the player, then it would have had a far greater chance of compliance with the rules rather than driving financial dealings underground all over again.

What to Charge and Who Pays

I've touched upon the reluctance of footballers to pay earlier but I still have to come to the unpleasant (or pleasant depending on who is looking at it) part of your job – charging your client. Sportspeople generally subscribe to the well-established showbiz tradition, namely that you should be prepared to work (or at least be available) 24/7 purely for the pleasure of knowing them. There are, of course, exceptions (and if any of my clients complain when they read this I intend to tell them that they are the exceptions).

Some clients are polite and grateful but, all too often, you can expect calls on your mobile with the caller launching into their problems, oblivious to the fact that you may be at dinner, at the theatre, in a meeting, asleep, at a funeral or even possibly dealing with some other client's affairs. The opening line, 'Is this a convenient time to talk?' is almost unheard of in the sports industry, as is any enquiry about your health. I treasure the memory of coming home after a fairly serious operation and being greeted by a footballer calling me whose first words were, 'The thing is, I don't know where I am supposed to be going for my trial…'

Still, you get used to it and if you want to keep your clients you do, at least, have to pretend to be polite and interested in their problems even if you are listening to them against the background of the cries of your newborn baby in a maternity ward.

But you have to make a living and you have to get paid by somebody. Football regulations (as I have mentioned) on the face of it do actually say that it is against the rules for a club to make any payments to anybody but the player or to anybody except on the player's behalf. A subtle difference but with the same tax consequences. Consequently, if you are able to persuade a club to pay your client an additional sum for the services you have rendered to your client (and there is no real reason why they should, other than the fact that your client thinks they should) then payment will be treated as a benefit in kind as far as the client is concerned and should be included in their P11D as just that. What has happened is that the club has made the payment to you on behalf of your client and not on its own behalf.

As The FA Regulations say that only a player can pay his agent the only way you can relieve him of that burden is by persuading his club to pay him a signing-on fee which equates to your agency fee (plus VAT which neither the club nor the player will be able to recover) grossed up with tax so it nets down to your fee. I am not an accountant but to achieve a net fee of say £10,000 plus VAT, namely £11,750 the club will have to pay the player about £18,000. The club will also have to pay Employer's National Insurance Contributions so all in all the 10k they would previously have happily (or not so happily paid you) now costs them £20,000. There are quite a few Premier League clubs who are regretting ever voting for this new approach to fees as if an agent has choices of clubs he is simply going to push his client in the direction of the one which is going to be most flexible about fees and ensure that his client doesn't really have to pay him anything, or will even take him abroad to a country where clubs do still pay agents' fees.

There are still problems as signing-on fees have to be paid in equal instalments and although the football agent can charge a lump sum in advance there seems to be no way of getting that money from the club as outlined above. Payments can be by lump sum or periodical payments either in advance or in arrears and weekly, monthly, quarterly or annually. There is one exception to the player paying his agent insofar as the player can direct the club to deduct the payments from his wage packets. Yet again The FA has offered little or no protection to the agent because such authority is not irrevocable and consequently once the player has seen for a couple of months that he is paying his agent's gross fees plus VAT out of his net income he may well just tell the club to stop paying and try and renegotiate with his agent. And if you are his agent then your cash flow goes out of the window,

The effect of payment of your fees by the club on the player's authority has to be explained to them (often several times) because otherwise you will get a call a month or so down the line asking you to contact their club because they haven't received enough salary (i.e. the club has deducted the relevant tax from the benefit in kind payment). In the good old days as long as you made it clear that they had a 100% obligation to you to pay your fees and you had reduced that effectively to 40% (or whatever their tax rate may be), then they were grateful. But those days are now gone and although as I have mentioned The FA and The AFA have instructed high powered tax accountants to try to get the Revenue to agree to treat footballers like entertainers and permit their agents' fees to be tax allowable that is not going to happen overnight (nor quite possibly in my lifetime).

The whole subject of fees in respect of playing contracts in football is a minefield. Obviously you shouldn't be receiving fees from both parties as a clear conflict-of-interest situation immediately arises. The client should always know what they are being charged or, indeed, what you are being paid if it is coming from a third party (which of necessity now is illegal and a breach of The FA Regulations but I can still see happening). If you don't tell them and the club suddenly decides to put it on their P11D with the relevant deduction, then they will have a nasty surprise and so will you when they send you a letter of termination, as well as a request for repayment of at least some of the fees you have received. What may also happen is if you get too clever and never register your agreement with the player and then 'act' for the club. The FA may decide that you really negotiated the deal for the player and the club may then be forced to reverse the transaction and charge the player the tax on what they paid you which is unlikely to endear you to your client.

I understand what The FA is trying to do as there have been some awful instances in the past. One well-known footballer was told by his agent that he was going to be charged full commission for a substantial transfer. He was then told that the agent would charge a slightly reduced fee and he was delighted and settled down to play at his new club, thinking his agent was the bee's knees. He then discovered, to his horror, a couple of months into his contract that he had received virtually no salary because a huge benefit in kind appeared on his pay-slip. This was the fee the agent had agreed with the club and, together with what he had charged the player, the agent came out with a six-figure sum although he didn't come out of the transaction with the client. The only thing now is that The FA have jumped the gun and if it had waited until The Revenue was on board then everybody would have accepted the situation.

Hold on a bit. I'm supposed to be talking about the charging provisions within the contract. The fact is that, to many representatives, what they are entitled to charge pursuant to their fee arrangement in their management contract is as relevant as the Declaration of Independence might have been to Stalin. But you are a good agent so what should you be charging?

To a large extent it is going to depend on the sport. Tennis and golf agents may charge up to 25% but quite often they have either just one client or supply their clients with a single dedicated representative. World-class golfers justify their own management structure and will have their own cottage (or probably mansion) industry for merchandising, sponsorship and licensing activities. In cricket, the income levels outside of the international superstars are relatively small and because it is harder to get deals the charges tend to be higher to make it worth the agent's while. In the United Kingdom, the big money is in football so that is where much of the jiggery-pokery (I've always wanted to work that expression into a book) lies.

Basic agency charges in football range between 2% of guaranteed income to 10% of everything. The former is modest and professional; the latter is fairly outrageous. However, if the player has been properly advised and agreed to it then that is their problem – but to justify it you need to be bloody good at your job. Before season 2001/2002, the licensed football agent could calculate the whole value of the contract over its entire duration and charge their commission rate. This meant the player giving up a fairly sizeable chunk of their first signing-on fee.

Most players don't see their contracts through and when they move tend to lose sight of the fact that they have already paid out commission on money they have never received. Similarly, if they stay at the same club, they might get a new contract halfway through their initial contract upon which the agent will levy new commission charges, even though this involves an element of double-charging. However, because you will be a good agent, all you will do is charge on the amount of the uplift from the old contract which is the fair and proper thing to do. What is grossly unfair under The FA Regulations is a provision that if your contract with a player comes to an end, although he is obliged to continue paying you on contracts you have negotiated, the minute that playing contract ends or is renegotiated and the player does not use your services then your payments CEASE. You don't even get paid on what the player continues to get pursuant to your efforts. The new agent who did the new deal gets the benefit of being able to charge commission on all the income from the new contract, including the sums that were already there and which gave him the basis on which to build. The FA's response is that it's 'swings and roundabouts' a reply that is as unconvincing as it is unfair.

The Premier League in England has become neurotic about illegal payments to third parties emanating from agents' fees. The scenario is fairly obvious. A manager (or another club official) tells the player's agent that they will sign their player and approve payment of substantial fees to the agent provided they get a slice of them. No brown paper bag, no deal. The Premier League, with The Quest Investigation, have taken on the role of the little Dutch boy sticking their finger in the dyke. But the whole scheme is fatally flawed because if agents were breaching the old regulations blatantly and with impunity, why shouldn't they be even more blatant about breaching the new regulations?

What agents now have to do is give assurances and undertakings that they are not making any payments to anybody involved in the club. The honest ones will give that assurance without hesitation and the dishonest ones will give that assurance and promptly break it.

It is fair for commission in high-paying team sports, e.g. football, rugby etc, to relate only to guaranteed income but some agents take a percentage right across the board, i.e. signing-on fees, salary, appearance money, bonuses, relocation costs and even insurance premiums paid by the clubs on behalf of the player. This always strikes me as more than a little greedy, not to mention being a breach of both The FA Regulations and FIFA regulations and does of course mean players have to produce salary statements each month for the agent to be able to calculate the commission. If such practices come to the attention of The FA there is no doubt that disciplinary proceedings will follow. Up until a few years ago, many agents just took a high percentage of signing-on fees but outside the Premiership (and indeed inside the Premiership at certain clubs) signing-on fees are becoming a thing of the past and they may well disappear altogether. Many clubs find it difficult to make capital payments and even if they can afford it they don't want to have a long-term commitment hanging over their heads just in case they get relegated and have to embark on a cost-cutting exercise.

Similarly, because a player is entitled to be paid up all of their signing-on fees if they leave without requesting a transfer, this can make a significant dent in any transfer fee received.

As I have said, most footballers in the past expected you to try and get your fees from the club and some still do, albeit in a different way as described earlier. Some players still actually insist on a clause in their contract with you that their payment should be spread over the period of the contract and even be paid on a monthly basis. That is not ideal as there is some accounting/monitoring required but, if they are prepared to pay by standing order and they are a client you are keen to represent, then it need not be a deal-breaker. Others want only to pay you on net income (i.e. what they actually receive from the club after deduction of tax) and not on gross income and, again, there is some argument that this may not be unfair although it's tricky to calculate and to monitor.

In representing an athlete in contract negotiations, you have to take into account the fact that the playing contract (or indeed the merchandising contract) that you negotiate may well outlive your representation contract. You may have done the best deal in the world for your client but that doesn't necessarily mean that they will appreciate it sufficiently to want to renew their contract with you. The grass is always greener on the other side (otherwise how would you get your clients?) so you have to be a bit philosophical about clients rolling on and off your players' roster.

But if you have got your client a great five-year playing contract or sponsorship deal, it is again very unfair that someone else should benefit from it after you have been unfairly and unreasonably dumped. So you need a clause clearly stating that, in the event of your contract expiring or being terminated, you will continue to receive commission on deals concluded by you. That seems to conflict with The FA Regulations and they may not register an agreement with such a clause but I am not sure that it is unenforceable in law.

There is a grey area in respect of deals that are under negotiation but not concluded. There is no hard and fast rule about this but what may be regarded as fair is that you should be entitled to commission at a reduced rate where, 'You've started but not finished'. The exception to this, in your favour, should be where you have brought a sponsorship deal to the table and in that case I can see no reason why you shouldn't be entitled to your full commission. However, on the flip side, if your client has terminated your contract for cause (i.e. because you are no damn good or have been dishonest) then there is no reason why you should continue to earn from their income. Again in football The FA will resist this though goodness knows why it is any of its business.

I explain termination clauses on both sides a little bit later but if your management contract expires or if there is mutual termination, then it seems to be only right and proper that your client should pay up any outstanding balances due to you. It is one thing allowing your client to owe you money and not charging interest when you are acting for them, quite another when they have moved on. Agents have to live too and as the reader is probably finding out, it's not all champagne, roses and million-pound deals for the great majority of them.

 In fact, you might want to include an enforceable penalty clause that if payments aren't made on time then you are entitled to charge interest. If you get really peeved with your client because they have acted so badly and they have unilaterally grabbed credit off you because they have bought themselves a new sports car or a luxury mansion (yes, generally speaking your payments come last), then your parting shot can be to send them a fresh invoice with the added interest.

Percentages for non-playing contracts are generally much higher. The reason for this is that sportspersons are usually offered contracts for playing by their employers and it is up to you to improve them. If you lean over backwards to be fair, then there is an argument for saying that you should only be allowed to charge on the uplift you actually secure in the same way as a mid-contract renegotiation. The odd player may actually come to you with that sort of deal – they have an offer from their club with which they are not happy and want you to try and improve it, but only want you to charge on the improvement.

However, that doesn't usually happen and you do charge on the whole contract. The sponsorship/marketing/licensing deals are different. Generally the agent will have sourced them, worked hard at getting them and even harder at negotiating them. I'm talking about income that your client simply wouldn't have had if you hadn't got it for them and I am also talking about compensation for efforts that haven't produced any end result upon which commission might have been charged. I'll deal with what ought to be included in those commercial contracts in the relevant chapter, but right now let's just consider what you can and should charge. I always think 20% is a reasonable benchmark although on higher figures you might want to reduce that to 10% or even less. A sliding scale might be appropriate; for example 20% on figures up to £500,000 (that'll earn you £100,000 in case you have great potential as an agent but none as a mathematician), 10% on the next £500,000 up to £1,000,000 (another £50,000 in the bank) and 5% after that. You have to be realistic and accept that for every £1,000,000 sponsorship deal there are hundreds of £100 interviews for which you make ten phone calls just to earn £20.

It is important to be seen to be fair to your client and, whether or not you are a solicitor, you should offer to open a separate client account to retain clients' money. Depending upon how long you are going to keep it, you might also want to pay interest on any deposits over a certain amount. It can be complicated and costly to account but, unless you are running a huge business, it is probably easier just to agree to send any monies you receive on to your client (after deduction of your commission) within seven days. Accounting quarterly is more in keeping with the music business or the publishing industry and if you are acting for sportspeople they are not likely to be as patient as musicians or writers. Certainly now in football you are obliged under The FA Regulations to send a statement of account once a year in September.

Even if you are accounting on a weekly basis, you don't really want to prepare accounts each week and therefore you should be willing to send a detailed account, say, quarterly and at the same time give your clients all the supporting documentation,
e.g. invoices you have raised to sponsors, royalty or commission

statements from licensees, detailed disbursements you are expending on their behalf, etc. Whether or not they read it (and I have to say from experience that it is more likely that their partner will go through it) is not your problem. If there is a falling-out later or a parting of the ways, you don't want to give either your erstwhile client or any new representative ammunition to use against you.

Go even further than providing the information and give the sportspersons the right to inspect your books either directly themselves or through their accountant. Limit it to a maximum of once or twice a year, as the last thing you want is a difficult client with time on his hands crawling all over your office to discover that you have under-accounted to him for £2.50. Give yourself a tolerance regarding accuracy of the accounts (5% is reasonable) but, quite frankly, if you are more than 5% out then you deserve all the flak you get. If I were acting for the client then I would be advising them to look to you for the cost of any audit that turns up a discrepancy in excess of 5% and for that particular audit not to count as one of the authorised inspections. If it were more than 10%, then I would be advising them to be looking for a new representative. As I have said before and will say again, honesty and full information are essential requirements for the good agent.

One thing you should be sure to put into any management contract is a limitation on how far clients can delve into your records. Yes, they should have full information about themselves but they should have zero access to any information about anybody else. If you have a couple of clients who know each other and one goes in to check their accounting and discovers how much you have earned for the other, then you only need client one to tell client two and the odds are that you will lose both of them. One because you have not earned him as much money and the other because his friend now knows exactly how much you have earned him. It is not unusual for clients in the same sport or at the same club to come and see you together for the sake of travelling convenience, but ensure you actually talk to them separately and, if they do insist on

More on the
Management Contract

I have dealt with all the good, positive stuff but what happens when things start to get frayed at the edges and you or your client want to part company? When I first left private practice as a solicitor and began to run a sports management company to which clients were actually contracted, I used to insert a clause stating that either party could terminate on one month's notice. I was used to a culture of loyalty within the legal profession where, provided you had done a good job, your client not only continued to instruct you but tended to recommend you to their friends and acquaintances.

I soon realised that the world of sports representation was a far cry from the non-poaching, non-solicitation world of the legal profession. Almost before the ink was dry on a contract, half a dozen agents would be phoning your new client to tell him that paradise was on their side of the fence and that they already had a club or commercial opportunity for him which only they could deliver – and could only deliver if he terminated his contract with me. So, several 'Dear John' letters later from clients for whom I had been ready, willing and able to sell my soul, I decided there had to be another way.

In the world of football, as I have mentioned (more than once), your representation contract can't be more than two years in duration and I have tended to adopt that period in relation to all sports. However, whilst a football representation contract can't be capable of extension beyond two years, this doesn't apply to other sports or indeed a contract in respect of commercial matters. Consequently, I apply the formula upon which I touched before, namely that when you reach an earnings level for the client (either over the two years or an average), then you should be entitled to exercise an option for the renewal of your contract. The renewal would contain the same option clause but with, for example, a 10% uplift on the amount you have to raise to be sure of keeping the client.

During each two-year period, the client should be entitled to terminate if you are in breach. I may be speaking to the initiated but there are two kinds of breaches, those that can be remedied and those that can't. If they can be remedied without any damage, there is no reason why the contract should be ended. Everyone makes mistakes. Let's take the example of you forgetting to send your quarterly statement of account on the due date. The client may want to get out of the contract, and might be waiting for you to step even fractionally off the straight and narrow. He knows the account is overdue and doesn't even bother to call you to point out your oversight, so he just zaps in with his termination letter. But if clients have to give you notice of the breach then obviously it is something that is easily remedied. You just say, 'Whoops!', beat your accounts department about their collective head and send the client his figures. Breach remedied and the client – you hope – is happy.

But if, say, you have a big sponsorship deal land on your desk with a time limit on it for acceptance and you forget to answer and the sponsor does their deal with another sportsperson, then you have irretrievably lost those funds and that opportunity for your client. If that is the case then not only should your client be allowed to terminate their contract with you but you might well also be liable to compensate him for damage loss.

Just a small point: make sure that the address for service of notice is correctly given. If you are a limited company you may well have your registered office in the contract rather than your trading address. The registered office may be at your accountants and if they fail to send on a letter to you, or delay in doing so, then your time for responding might have run out by the time it actually gets to you.

The boot may be on the other foot if you, the agent, want to end the contract. Some clients prove to be either impossible or just plain bad news. You get the client a sponsored car and they can't even be bothered to roll out of bed to go and open a garage which is all they have to do to collect it. The garage or the advertising agency goes ballistic and refuses to deal with you again and thus all your other clients' opportunities have been prejudiced.

But back to the boots. One of the main points of complaint from potential sponsors (particularly with footballers) is that they are given vast amounts of freebies and then end up wearing rival companies' merchandise because they have either given their sponsor's gear away or just simply prefer the rival equipment. This can happen where one company is prepared to pay for a player to wear the boots and another company isn't, but your client prefers the latter's boots.

Boot companies are always on the look-out for breaches in respect of their sponsorship merchandise and nothing is likely to prove more irritating than one of your sponsored clients scoring an important goal wearing a competitor's footwear. There you have the goal shown over and over again on TV, pictured in the papers and the football magazines, exactly the sort of sponsorship opportunity for which the main sponsor has paid good money and they get nothing out of it. Whilst it is irrational for the boot company to blame you, you can bet your bottom dollar or top lira that they will.

Again, you will find yourself blacklisted and those odd favours you need from boot companies just won't be forthcoming. Not all of your clients will be superstars in demand and a relationship with a sportswear company that enables you to phone up and request a single pair of boots or trainers as a favour (even if you pay wholesale for them) is a vital part of your representative armoury. If you have lost that right because your client has chosen to blast several large holes through an agreement that's worth a lot of money to them (and not a little to you), then you have to ask yourself whether you really want to continue to act for that particular individual.

If you decide that a client is more of a liability than an asset and want to call it a day, you will have to think through the consequences. The fact that your client is a waste of space with regard to his commercial responsibilities doesn't mean that he is also a waste of space on the field of play. His club will still love him for the great goals he has scored with the unsponsored boots and offer him a new remunerative contract. He may still be a favourite with the fans who wish to buy his merchandise. You have decided to dump him because he has brought you into disrepute with the boot company but, because of his breach of his (and your) contracts, why should you continue to lose out on his on-the-pitch income?

Unscrupulous players may well be delighted that you have terminated and that they can now move on to an equally unscrupulous agent. What you should therefore insert in your contract is a clause that states that if you terminate for cause and the player enters into a new playing contract or gets a transfer within a certain period after termination, then he still has to pay you, for example, full commission for 90 days and then 50% for another 30 or 25% for another 60 days. It is not perfect and, of course, it does require a certain amount of policing, but it is as good as it gets. Mind you, it is doubtful if The FA will agree to that sort of clause going into your representation contract so you may have to insert it into the commercial contract between the company and the player, a contract that may still be outside the reaches of The FA though they may believe otherwise,

One thing that is perfectly fair is that if, at the end of a contract, the player still has outstanding fees to pay, those should be paid up immediately. As I mentioned before, it is one thing being an interest-free banker to an existing client, quite another to extend the facility to someone who has moved on to be represented by someone else.

It is possible that an athlete who is successful off the pitch may at some stage form their own image company. By this I mean a limited company which is substantially owned by the sportsperson but which, in turn, owns the rights to that sportsperson's image and thus also the rights to his commercial activities.

Without going into all the gory legal details, the sportsperson will formally transfer his image (and his nickname, signature, caricature etc.) into a limited company which may or may not be wholly owned by him. Sometimes his or her significant other will have a stake; sometimes his management company will have shares. Whichever may be the case, he will probably enter into a service contract (like a contract of employment) with the service company under which he will agree to fulfil any contract that the image company enters into on his behalf. Where a partner is in a lower tax bracket, this can be quite a tax-effective way of diverting income provided the partner does provide some genuine services (e.g. secretarial) to the company.

However, where does that leave you, the agent, if the sportsperson follows his accountant's or lawyer's advice and goes the image company route? You have a contract with your individual client for 20% (give or take) of their commercial income but suddenly he doesn't have any commercial income because he has given it all away to his image company. All you get (at best) is 20% (give or take) of whatever the image company deigns to pay him because the person with whom you have contracted no longer has any direct commercial income himself. And you'll get nothing of any monies paid to the partner as mentioned above.

The way to deal with it is for the client to be restricted in any assignment of those rights (i.e. not to be able to transfer them without your consent as the manager). They may argue that is too restrictive so you would then say that your consent can't be withheld so long as the client ensures that the image company enters into a contract with you, the manager, to pay the same amount of commission that you would have earned under your own individual management contract. Don't forget you are not then limited by the two-year restriction, as commercial contracts are not bound by The FA Regulations unless they are between the agent individually and the player. Indeed, as I have already said, you could have two contracts with your clients, one in relation to their playing activities (limited to two years) and one in relation to their commercial activities (for a longer period of time). As far as football is concerned then the commercial one needs to be with a limited company unless you are not concerned that The FA can not only potentially delve into it but also possibly use it to stop you acting for a club in relation to a player you have represented commercially. The argument in your favour for that would be that it does take a fair amount of time to develop commercial activities and two years is simply insufficient.

Whilst you want to keep any management contract as simple and short as possible, there are still a few more clauses that, in their own little way, are as important as any of the charging clauses.

Ensure that the client acknowledges that they are neither employed by you, nor in partnership with you and undertakes that they will be responsible for their own personal tax, any National Insurance contributions (relevant if they are employed by their own image company) and VAT (relevant if they are wildly successful).

It may seem obvious but, as mentioned earlier, you do want your client to warrant that he doesn't have any other current management contracts that might conflict with your agreement. Due to a mix of naïveté and conventional memory loss, it is not unknown for a sportsman to enter cheerfully into a management contract with you before his contract with a third party has expired or whilst, even more cheerfully, ignoring any option that his previous manager may have. The other side of the coin is to ensure that your client treats you in the same way and confirms that your agreement will be their only valid management contract for the relevant period. In this respect please note carefully my earlier comments about the registration of football representation playing contracts.

Then there is the question of confidentiality. The last thing that you (and probably your client) want is for any sounding-off in the press about the agreement or any matter arising from it. The confidentiality clause is probably more in favour of the client than the agent. He won't want you telling the world the details of any deal you get him just so you can prove what a great agent you are. On the other hand, you won't want him giving any details of your business or indeed even what you charge them. You certainly won't want them giving any details about whatever it was that caused the pair of you to break up. You may well have different rates for different clients or even for different sports, and if one of your clients finds out you have charged him 5% whilst another has been charged 3%, he won't be a happy bunny. If you do have a dissatisfied client – whether or not the dissatisfaction is justified – you don't want him going public to tell the world the causes of his dissatisfaction.

Finally (yes, I have actually got to the end of the contract), you do have to be sure that your clients have been fully and properly advised as to the contents and effect of the management contract. So how do you do that? Well, you can take them by the hand and lead them to the lawyer, which is what often happens in the music industry. Pop music managers have seen a whole stream of cases setting aside management contracts either because of undue influence or because the contract is so unfair as to be burdensome. Both these causes are usually supported by the fact that a young naïve musician has not been given the opportunity to take independent legal advice.

Now, in the real world, it is simply not possible always to satisfy yourself that a young footballer has taken your contract and shown it to a solicitor. Very often, the best you can hope for is that they get their parents to read it and they raise a couple of points. However, you have to be seen to be doing the right thing and you must put in writing the very strong simple advice that what they are about to sign is a very important document and not only should they read it carefully before signing, but they should take independent advice (preferably from a solicitor) and that you will consider any amendments either they or their solicitors or other advisors may request. The FA, as I've said, has standard wording and clauses for this as you will see from the precedents on their website and, indeed, my approved precedent. In relation to other sports you need to cover your back equally carefully. There is nothing so frustrating than discovering a young golfer, seeing him turn into a world champion and then allowing him to get out of your contract because you didn't ensure that he got independent advice.

To protect yourself, the magic words you should use are: 'The player/sportsperson/athlete/sportswoman [delete whichever doesn't apply – all of them if you are managing a personality racehorse like Red Rum or Desert Orchid, I suppose] confirms that he/she/it has read and understood the terms contained in the agreement and that prior to signing this agreement, he has been advised to and has taken independent legal advice in respect of them'. If you can find out the name of the lawyer from whom the advice has been taken, so much the better. And if they say they have and they haven't...? If this was a book written for the music industry, I might be more cautious but, as far as the sports world is concerned, you can do no more. You have been seen to be doing the right thing and hopefully you will always continue to do the right thing.

Agent or Lawyer?

Agent or lawyer? Or both? Or can one and the same person be one and the same thing? Whilst the title of this book is how to be a sports agent, the fact of the matter is that sports agency work is now attracting more and more lawyers and the questions I have asked pose philosophical, moral and commercial problems as well as those of a strictly legal nature.

In many instances, a sportsperson will appoint an agent who will in turn appoint a lawyer to deal with the legal documentation that the representation of a successful sportsperson will generate. But whose lawyer are they? Are they duty-bound to look beyond the merchandising or sponsorship contract upon which they have been asked to advise and to examine the whole structure of the relationship between the agent and the sportsperson? Is it possible or, indeed, correct for the lawyer to put on their blinkers and ignore what they may perceive as irregularities or indiscretions by the agent 'above the line', so to speak?

There can be several examples of this. Many sports agents have a background in insurance. Many of them are tied agents, unable to give independent advice but only able to give advice on particular products marketed by one particular company, and are therefore unable to provide the client with a choice of insurance products. If the lawyer is present while the agent 'sells' their sporting client a policy, do they have an obligation to point out that the client should compare the product with others on the market? Do they have to ensure that the sportsperson actually reads the documentation, setting out the amount of commission being earned by the agent, or must they remain silent and loyal to the agent who has instructed them?

Similarly, if the lawyer considers, from their commercial awareness of the market place, the net amount available to the player, after deduction of the agent's 20% commission, in relation to a commercial deal is insufficient and compares unfavourably with that achieved for other players, should he say so?

Wearing my lawyer's hat, the answer to all of these questions is a resounding yes. I firmly believe that the lawyer's duty to the public as a whole, let alone their duty to an individual with whom they have fallen into a 'semi-client' relationship, overrides the pure solicitor/client relationship. So if you, as an agent, have taken your client to a lawyer who has a problem, should the lawyer gracefully bow out, saying they have a conflict or do they risk the breach of a solicitor/client confidentiality by telling the sportsperson exactly what they feel about the actions, inactions or non-disclosure by the agent and their erstwhile client? I personally believe the lawyer should tell all although I suspect that both The SRA and negligence insurers might disagree with me.

For this reason, the solicitor must not fall into the trap of doing nothing because the situation may rebound on them. Players, by the very nature of their profession, drift from advisor to advisor. An agent operating successfully at one football or rugby club or county cricket club in the south may well act for a player on their transfer to a northern club or county where a rival agent is firmly entrenched. Players inevitably talk among themselves about their income and their advisors. A player, therefore, in a different environment may instruct another agent who, in reviewing the job their predecessor has done, will similarly review the lawyer's involvement and performance. Agents are a breed very like builders. When asked to look at a contract negotiated by somebody else, much head-shaking goes on as do 'oohs' and 'ahs' of disbelief and the inevitable comment ('You mean you actually paid for this advice?') and, whilst indemnity insurance is now compulsory for agents under the new regulations, a lawyer is still a much more attractive target. As far as football is concerned a representation contract between a Registered Lawyer and a player must also now contain a clause pursuant to which a player can represent himself in any contract negotiation. That hardly encourages loyalty or provides security because, although as I have mentioned you can provide for your fees to be paid even though the player represents himself, it is not always about money but also about protection of reputation. And it does your street cred no good whatsoever if your players are running off and doing deals themselves and then renegotiating their fees with you from a position of strength.

The agent/lawyer partnership has to involve the lawyer's total satisfaction that the agent is acting solely in the interest of the client, which is difficult (although not impossible) considering the commission arrangement. There are agents (and I hope you will be one of them) who will advise against entering into a contract (even if this costs them their commission) when they believe the contract is not a good one for the client.

I used to think there was little or nothing an agent could do that a lawyer couldn't and, in theory, that is probably the case. However, the current level of charging rates means that it is simply not cost-effective for a lawyer to spend speculative time for sportspeople in seeking TV appearances, clothing deals and media work generally. If a sports magazine is paying £100 for an article that takes a couple of hours to set up, the lawyer's charges may well amount to £800 plus VAT! Lawyers have only one commodity to sell, their time, which must be used constructively and sparingly, otherwise their clients will become disenchanted.

I don't agree with The FA's definition of 'permitted legal advice' nor the fact that they believe it is necessary to regulate lawyers who negotiate playing contracts (it's what we do for a living, for heaven's sake) but if you are a lawyer reading this then do familiarise yourself with The FA Regulations insofar as they relate to you to avoid problems not only with The FA themselves but also The SRA to whom they are entitled to report you. Oh, Brave New World.

In the music business, it is quite common for a record company to pay for their new artists' lawyer's fees, to ensure that they get independent advice and it may well be that you, as an agent earning potentially substantial commission, will feel this is appropriate as well. If the lawyer is acting on their own without involving an agent, then they have to take onboard the fact that the career-guidance element is a loss leader and be prepared to accept an element of speculation and investment. The 18-year-old Paul Gascoigne, whom I began to represent in 1985, was not the marketable product which emerged from Italia '90 and those five years required faith and patience. For every Gascoigne there are a hundred young wannabes who will fade into oblivion. Gazza's subsequent decline without the benefit of my advice is a matter of great sadness to me.

What I am saying is that if you are not a lawyer yourself, use a lawyer, pick them wisely and do not give them a reason either to withdraw from a transaction because of conflict or to lose you any of your clients. Rather, use them as a partner in developing a business which is to your mutual benefit.

Keeping the Client

So now you are all set up. You have a management structure, you have a trusted professional advisor (if you are not a professional yourself) and you have clients. You now have the biggest headache of them all – what to do with them and how to keep them happy.

The way to deal with the latter is to make sure you don't get greedy and take on too many clients without an infrastructure to service them. If you have one client you can phone him half a dozen times a day to make sure he knows you are thinking of him and him alone (you can overdo it too – so make sure you don't drive the client mad by phoning him and gibbering on about nothing at all). With just that one client you can also be sure that if he wants to get hold of you, you will always be there for him. Life is simple. You can ask kit companies for favours because you are only requesting one pair of boots or trainers, one tracksuit, one pair of gloves. But can you make any money out of it? The answer is probably no, unless you are representing an Andy Murray, a Tiger Woods, a David Beckham, a Wayne Rooney, a Lewis Hamilton or the like.

Even if you were to represent exclusively one leading athlete from the somewhat less commercial sports, such as hockey, show-jumping or weight-lifting, you would probably struggle to make a living.

So you take on a few more clients and suddenly you are only calling the six you act for once a day, then there's a dozen and it's once or twice a week until you have thirty or forty and then you suddenly find yourself needing to take on someone else. This is a problem in itself. Can you trust them? Will the players like them? Are you able to delegate? Are they going to steal all your clients?

This wasn't meant to be one of those little self-help books which have a single piece of advice per page with a little cartoon that makes you want to heave both the book and the writer out of a 20-storey window. However, delegation, trust and efficiency are key words when you are running a sports agency. When you get to the point of taking on an assistant it is likely to be either someone young and ambitious – a wannabe Jerry Maguire – or else an athlete from the sport in which you specialise. Track and field athletes are invariably managed by an ex-athlete and most football agencies either directly or indirectly employ an ex-professional player who, in theory, speaks the language of the client.

But what do you do if your clients get too close to your assistant? What do you do if he becomes the first port of call for them? And what do you do if he gets headhunted by another agency or decides to leave and set up on his own? One vital step is to get him to sign a non-competition clause within the agreement when you employ him. Don't draft it yourself – get it prepared by your trustworthy solicitor. They are difficult to enforce and courts generally lean in favour of the employee rather than the employer. There is a presumption against restraint of trade (i.e. stopping somebody carrying on their business, particularly if it is the only business they know) which is becoming ever stronger as we move further into Europe. The restrictions that can be enforced are limited but at least it will make a rogue assistant think twice before he tries to walk away with all your clients. Again, in view of The FA Regulations I have to refer you to the provisions in representation contracts as to what happens when the agent who has signed the contract leaves your organisation. You may well prefer to allow him to represent the client so long as he continues to account to you for monies received for so long as you would have been entitled to benefit had he not left, otherwise, if a client doesn't want you to act for him, you'll find it nearly impossible to prevent your ex-employee representing him.

Hopefully, if you make it known to his new prospective employers (assuming that he is going to work for someone else rather than set up on his own) that such a restrictive covenant exists, then they may well not want to take on potential litigation and at least you will be making it hard for your man to find meaningful employment elsewhere. The new employer may also think that if their prospective employee has stabbed you in the back, there is no reason why he won't do it to them at some stage.

That's the legal remedy but the more practical remedy is to delegate intelligently. Keep in touch with all your clients yourself. Get your assistant (or assistants, as you continue to expand) to fill in report sheets telling you when they speak to each of your clients, what they said to them, what they were asked or offered to do and whether they have done it. Get particularly nervous when the client allegedly isn't calling back. If you make one call to every three your assistant makes, then the proportion is probably right, but make it clear to the client that you still make all the decisions, that nothing goes on in the business without you knowing about it (hence the necessity for the report sheets) and that you are still in control of negotiating all of your client's contracts. Once again you have to tread carefully with The FA in football if you give your unauthorised staff anything more than administrative duties to carry out.

If the client realises you are interested in them and also realises that whilst your assistant does the day-to-day administration, you call all the shots, then you have a realistic chance of keeping the client even if you have staff changes. It is hard to generalise because the sports world is full of stories about assistants, solicitors or even lawyers who have worked with an established sports agent, taken in all the information like a sponge and then walked away with enough clients to set up their own business. Unfortunately, life is like that and the world of sports management is even more like that. All you can do is the right thing and recognise when others are doing the wrong thing.

Apart from keeping in touch regularly, the best way to keep your clients happy is to find work for them and when you have found the work (or the work has found you), then to negotiate the best deal you can. Now, that all sounds terribly simple and it is, in a way, if you have a hot property. If the client is a footballer, clubs will be falling over themselves to sign him. If he is a tennis player or a golfer, invitations to tournaments will be filling up your in-tray. And as for the sponsors, the advertising agencies and the media, well they will be beating a path to your door. The trick is to find the clubs, the opportunities and the deals for your B- and C-list clients and, believe me, that is neither easy nor simple.

In terms of the contracts that will come your way to negotiate, these fall generally into the following categories:

- Playing contracts, tournament contracts and generally on-pitch or in-sport agreements.
- Contracts to represent clubs in buying or selling players or arranging friendly matches.
- Sponsorship deals involving athletic kit relating specifically to your client's sport, i.e. endorsements.
- More general merchandising contracts including own-brand deals, e.g. a leisure clothing range or sunglasses.
- General endorsements on television, in the cinema, on posters, in papers, e.g. the use of the client's image in an advertisement for a car or a credit card.
- Media contracts, e.g. one-off interviews, regular columns, own TV show.
- Publishing contracts, skill books, authorised biographies, autobiographies.
- Personal appearances, e.g. after-dinner speaking, opening shops, fêtes, garages.
- Big-screen/record contracts, which are only for the superstars and a bit too esoteric and specialised to be dealt with here.
- Internet agreements, the creation, monitoring and commercial utilisation of a player's own website.

I will deal with as many of these areas as space allows in the following chapters.

Playing Contracts –
The Principles

You have a licence and an office. You have some clients who have signed an acceptable form of management (or in football a representation agreement) contract and now you are faced with your next big challenge – you have to get them some paid work or, in the case of most athletes, get them better paid work than they had when you made your pitch to secure the right to represent and exploit them. This is crunch time. You have to perform. The only problem (or at least the main problem) is that you can't perform if they don't perform.

The mantra I always chant to prospective clients is, 'You have to do it on the pitch if I am to do anything for you off the pitch'. (There you are – when I agreed to write the book, I told the publishers I wasn't going to give away my trade secrets, and I have just gone and given the equivalent to 'Number 42' from *The Hitchhiker's Guide To The Galaxy*.)

I will look at on-the-field playing contracts for the clients before considering off-the-pitch sponsorship or endorsements. I could fill a dozen books with analysis of playing contracts but they wouldn't be very interesting so I have decided to focus on some popular UK sports and give a thumbnail sketch of what you can expect to find in them, and what you can hope to negotiate in them.

If you thought I was going to start with football, then you are right. It's not that I am biased. It's just that, certainly as far as the UK is concerned, it is the most common contract between a sportsman and his employer, probably the most remunerative on average and the one you are most likely to come across. It is also a good starting place for comparisons because, as you will see, the balance of negotiating power gradually (or at times dramatically) slips from employee to employer as you move across from football to rugby and then to cricket. The football-playing contract is a good template to work from and, although other less affluent sports such as cricket and rugby may try to resist having footballing clauses inserted in their standard contracts, there is no harm in trying. As my grandmother used to say, 'If you don't ask, you don't get'.

Most sports have a standard form of playing contract drafted by its governing body, often in conjunction with the relevant players' union. That doesn't mean they are perfect and it also doesn't mean that you, as the agent, don't need to bother to read them. Often a seemingly innocuous clause can lead to a negligence action if you don't get it taken out or amended, or don't tell your client about its effect if it has to stay in. It is always best to treat a contract as if you were a solicitor (even if you are not) and the player as a client buying a house or taking the lease of a shop.

It is sometimes not enough to go through the contract in detail either over the phone or face to face. The player may deny you did it or claim they simply didn't understand it (probably quite true, in some cases). To be on the safe side, it is always best to put your 'report' on the contract in writing, explaining it clause-by-clause in the simplest language. Sometimes there simply isn't time for this when you are summoned to a meeting and the club insists that the agreement is knocked out that day, signed and the player is registered in time for an important match, but do try.

I am not being condescending but the fact of the matter is that you are probably not dealing with a sophisticated streetwise businessman. In many cases your client is a kid of 20 or younger who is about to earn money beyond his wildest dreams, whilst his contemporaries are stacking shelves in supermarkets. He probably left school at 16 and may not even have a single GCSE, even in woodwork. It has to be simple and it has to be clear.

After the first edition of this book, what came to be known as 'the Bosman Rule' changed the face of football contracts forever and led to FIFA changing their own regulations to accommodate the new-found freedom of contract and compensatory payments. Without going into enormous detail, what you must keep in mind is that a player who is 24 and at the end of his playing contract can leave to go anywhere in the world without payment of any compensation to the club who employed him. A player who is 23 at the end of his contract can do the same provided he is going abroad and for that purpose it seems that a cross-border move from Scotland to England is sufficient. The recent case of Andy Webster may also be a benchmark in the battle for total freedom of contract.

Andy Webster used Article 17 of the FIFA Regulations to walk out on Heart of Midlothian in Scotland to move to Wigan Athletic in the English Premiership. Hearts looked for a substantial fee and eventually were awarded £625,000 by FIFA. The player appealed to the Court of Arbitration (CAS) who replaced that figure by a far more modest £150,000. Having established that a player can unilaterally terminate his contract where he has served at least three years of a four- or five-year contract provided he is 23-28 it is now clear that a player can walk away when he is 28 provided he has fulfilled at least two years of a contract. All of this has to be taken into account when you negotiate a football contract. Not just the monies, but also your client's age at various stages of the contract and, of course, the length of the contract itself.

The significance of this is that your client will not thank you if you have tied him in to a long contract that takes him well past the 'Bosman' date and doesn't allow him to escape pursuant to Article 17 and 'Webster'. He may want to leave his club at 24 with two years to go on his contract and the contract only being for three years to start with, and they may seek an extortionate fee for his release. They know he wants to leave and they also know that in a year's time they will get nothing for him. It is not quite that simple, of course. There are market forces which do, in practice, create checks and balances. No club wants to keep an unhappy player and there is a game of poker to be played in which you, as the agent, will have the advantage of seeing everybody's hand. An agent's role is not just to negotiate the terms of his client's contract; it is also to get to the point where such negotiations are possible. You have to accept that you cannot be all things to all parties in a transaction, you have to accept that somewhere along the line you may well upset somebody, but as long as you play it straight and do everything in the interests of your client, without lying or cheating, you will emerge with your reputation intact and, hopefully, a healthy commission cheque in your bank account.

Returning to the length of the contract that, in itself, Webster apart, is always a difficult balancing act. Do you go for security and take a long contract that may ultimately prejudice the player, or do you take your (and his) chances and ensure that his contract will end contemporaneously with him coming of Bosman age and gamble on him being in demand? If his career does not pan out the way you hope, then, with so many players (and agents) scurrying around to find clubs for ordinary players who are out of contract, you may find yourself doing a lot of work for very little reward. You may also find yourself losing a client as in desperation he turns to other agents who are busying themselves looking for players who will generate any income at all, however small.

The form of the Premier League contract has also changed since the first edition of this book, in 2002, and what complicates matters even further is that the Football League contract differs in many ways. There are still some minefields in both of them through which it is necessary to tiptoe. I don't have the time or space in a volume of this nature to do a clause-by-clause analysis of the whole contract and anyway my American readers are screaming out for me to talk about MLS (Major League Soccer that is) contract. The fact of the matter is that there are some specific problems inherent in that worthy document but, unless you're a superstar coming into the States, they're unlikely to accept too many amendments.

Clause 7.2 of the Premier League contract is worth considering. It says:

> In the event that the Player shall become incapacitated from playing by reason of any injury or illness (including mental illness or disorder) the Club shall pay to the Player during such period of incapacity or the period of this contract (whichever is the shorter) the following amounts of remuneration for the following periods:
>
> 7.2.1 In the case of a Player Injury [more about that later] his basic wage over the first 18 months and one half of his basic wage for the remainder of his period of incapacity;
>
> 7.2.2 In the case of any other injury or illness his basic wage over the first 12 months and one half of his basic wage for the remainder of his period of incapacity...

The crucial wording here is 'whichever is the shorter' because, I believe, to be fair, it should read 'whichever is the longer, but so as not to extend beyond 30 days from the end of the period of the contract'.

This would then mean that if your client gets ill he is effectively paid for the whole of the contract period and it will be up to the club to take out insurance to indemnify themselves against such a contingency.

This must be distinguished from permanent incapacity. During an illness (covered by 7.2) until it's proved to be a permanent incapacity the contract can't be terminated. However, Clause 8, which has replaced the old Clause 10 (and for those of you who have the first edition of this book and want to make comparisons, turn to Page 50 – if, indeed, you are reading the three editions side by side then you need to get out more) is a whole new ball game as far as serious, and possibly permanent, injury is concerned.

Let me say straightaway that what we have now is better than the old Clause 10. Having been banging away about this for years to anybody who would listen (and some who wouldn't), it does seem as if the football authorities in the UK have finally come around to my way of thinking. It just needs my wife to follow their example. However, unlike my wife, the clause is still not perfect.

There are definitions of 'Permanent Injury' on Page 3 of the contract. Even if you do not have a copy of the old edition of this book by your side I do, at least, expect you to have a copy of the Premier League contract and so, I do not intend setting that out in full... despite the temptation to do so in order to help me fulfil my publisher's word target! Mind you, I actually got a complaint letter about my book How to Complain (same publisher if you are minded to buy it) accusing me of padding out the book and asking for a rebate of part of the purchase price.

Clause 8 does also bring into play new definitions such as 'The Initial Opinion' and 'The Further Opinion', which may give you a clue as to its complexity. What actually happens now is that the Club thinks a player's career is finished and gets a medical opinion to that effect. They terminate the contract. The player has 21 days to request a second opinion, this time to be given by a doctor approved by him. If the two opinions conflict then, if the further opinion has been given by a doctor nominated by the President of the Royal College of Surgeons, it prevails. However, if it's been given by a doctor nominated by the player, then a third opinion from a doctor who is nominated by the aforementioned President will give the final decision.

And once that decision bites then Clause 8 kicks in and here it depends on whether the termination is for what's now called a 'Player Injury', which is an injury sustained other than pursuant to a breach of the playing contract, or another sort of injury, e.g. one which is caused by getting involved in a dangerous activity such as skiing, go-carting or motor cycling, etc.

Again, holding the thought of how the doctor's opinion works, the way a club can react to a player injury is to get the first opinion and then terminate the contract. Even without the opinion it can still terminate if the player has been unable to play for 18 months in any 20-month period. The length of the notice is 12 months if it's a Player Injury and 6 months if it's not.

The medical hoops may take a little while to jump through, but if it's immediately apparent that a player's contract is at an end then a five-year contract can be terminated on a little over 18 months' notice.

Now let's examine a practical scenario to see the possible effect of that clause. You have a remarkable 19-year-old prospect in Joey Johnson. He signs a highly remunerative five-year contract with a Premiership club. You do everything right. You get him a substantial signing-on fee of, let's say, £500,000. Under the current rules in England, this has to be paid in equal instalments and normally there is one instalment per season (although there can be any number as long as they are equal in each year). You get him an attractive salary, which increases as the contract goes on, so let's say he starts at £5,000 per week but, by the end of the contract, he is on £20,000 per week. You get him all sorts of performance-related bonuses and maybe a huge loyalty bonus of £100,000 if he is still in the employ of the club at the end of the contract. (I'll deal with all these clauses in more detail a little later.)

But then, six months into the contract, after he has received just one instalment of the signing-on fee, Joey has his leg broken by a hulking defender. The injury is so bad that he is told that he will never play again. The club makes sympathetic noises, then realises that it has contracted to pay him a few million pounds over the next four-and-a-half years for doing nothing. It has probably insured him itself for its own benefit and, after a short period of mourning, it banks that money and then writes Joey a letter giving him 18 months' notice to terminate.

There is nothing in Clause 8 to say the club has an obligation to pay the balance of the signing-on fee. The player gets the lump sum disability benefit under the terms of The FA Premier League Personal Accident Insurance Scheme, which will in no way compensate him for the income he would have received under the playing contract or what he would have earned over the rest of his career.

It seems to me that, to avoid this outcome, you still have to do at least three things. One is to try and get the contract varied. The simplest way is to say that notice under this clause cannot be served prior to 19 months before the end of the contract. That would mean that your client would continue to be paid until 31 July (i.e. one month after his contract expires – all football contracts start on 1 July and end on 30 June) of the final year of his contract. However, at the end of the contract, if a player doesn't sign a new contract but hasn't found a new club, then his old club is bound to continue to pay him for an extra month.

If you cannot get the contract varied, then you have to ask the club if it will pay for insurance cover in a lump sum, with the club paying the player premiums annually or paying them on his behalf. The downside to this is that your client will be taxed on the premiums as a benefit in kind whilst the variation doesn't give rise to any such liability. The club may choose to cover its potential, reducing liability by insurance but it is not obliged to do so.

If the club turns around and says it will neither vary Clause 8 nor contribute to the insurance, then you can try a different tack and seek to compromise by saying that the club can't terminate at all if the injury is sustained whilst on club duty. Club duty can mean playing, training, travelling, even falling down the steps of the team coach (as long as he is not drunk at the time). You can even add a further spin to it (the job of a good sports agent is to be thinking on your feet continually and to negotiate until there is absolutely no further room to negotiate). This would mean to say that if the club is obliged to keep paying the player, then the player is similarly obliged to accept the offer of any job at the club which may be made to him at no extra remuneration; for example at a youth academy or in community liaison. He may even have to agree to go on a coaching course to obtain a certificate. It seems to me both from the point of view of the club and its employee to be absolutely fair and reasonable that an injured player who continues to be paid should not be allowed just to put his feet up and count the cash as it rolls in.

So there you have it, one little clause, all those problems, all those interpretations, all those potential solutions. Just how many agents, I wonder, even know that Clause 8 exists, or even bother to read through any sports playing contract from start to finish? It may well be that, with the changes in licensing regulations and the obligation to sit an exam, supported by indemnity insurance, rather than simply posting a bond, that the culture of sports representation may change a little, though I very much doubt it. Oh, a by the way, don't forget that if your client's contract with his club comes to an end then so do your payments.

Here is another problematic clause, Clause 3.2.4. This says:

> The Player agrees that he shall not undertake or be engaged in any other employment or to be engaged in any trade business or occupation... without the prior written consent of the Club PROVIDED THAT this shall not:
>
> 3.2.4.1 prevent the Player from making any investment in any business so long as it does not conflict or interfere with his obligations hereunder; or
>
> 3.2.4.2 limit the Player's rights under Clauses 4 and 6.1.8 (again you need to get the contract and cross-reference to them).

It seems fair, doesn't it? The club pays them a lot of money and they work exclusively for the club, which is not really going to want them to toddle off after training and go to help their dad out on a building site. But (there is always a but, isn't there?) you have already seen the list of marketing activities in which a player could be involved. As I mentioned before, he can incorporate a service company to own his image and, if he is a director of that company, he can receive remuneration to avoid having to dividend-out profits. The fact is that he is engaged directly (possibly) or indirectly (certainly) in a 'trade, business or occupation' which is most definitely 'other than his employment' under the playing contract. These are business opportunities that flow from the playing contract but are of a very different nature and variety. The establishment of his own service contract is very far from the mere making of an 'investment'. He will be the *raison d'etre* of the company and will be actively involved. As long as he always remembers his primary obligation comes first, why should he agree to accept any restrictions?

So, again, you have to lift your trusty pen, draw a line through the clause or else just add the words, 'other than in relation to any services that may be provided by the player to any service company which may own in whole or part the rights to his image, name, likeness, nickname or caricature in relation to the licensing, marketing and merchandising of the same'.

The odds are that whoever you are dealing with at the club will try and resist this amendment, largely because clubs are becoming more and more switched on themselves as far as marketing opportunities are concerned. It wants to keep all the image rights, have players on its website rather than let them set up their own and use their image to promote club merchandise in the club catalogue, rather than permit the player and his agent to get what deals they can in the commercial arena. Indeed, if you look at Clause 4.4 you will see that:

> The Player agrees that he will not either on his own behalf or with or through any third party undertake promotional activities in a Club Context nor exploit the Player's Image in a Club Context in any manner and/or in any Media nor grant the right to do so to any third party.

Just look at the very wide drafting of the definition of 'Club Context':

> ...in relation to any representation of the Player and/or the Player's Image a representation in connection or combination with the name colours Strip trade marks logos or other

identifying characteristics of the Club (including trade marks and logos relating to the Club and its activities which trade marks and logos are registered in the name of and/or exploited by any Associated Company) or in any manner referring to or taking advantage of any of the same.

Basically the Club wants to keep as much of the player's image rights as possible and make it as difficult as they can for you, his agent, to market him in a commercial and financially remunerative manner. You do need to try and renegotiate that and obviously the more high profile your client the more successful you are likely to be.

Apart from these pointers, how does the reputable and responsible sports agent go about negotiating an acceptable playing contract? Well, first of all, deal with your fees last, not first. All too often agents flounce into a meeting and after a brief 'Good morning' (not obligatory), will tell the club that their fee of £X,000 (think of a number and treble it) has to be paid or else there is no point in talking. And as we now know the only way you can get a club to pay your fees indirectly is to gross them up, plus VAT, as a signing-in fee or loyalty payment. Even then, by the way, there is no guarantee that once the club has paid the net figure to your client that he will pass it on. His wife may suddenly realise an urgent need for new curtains, carpets and furniture as the figure hits his bank account and he may plead poverty to you and ask for more time to pay.

The fact of the matter is that you have a contract with your client and under The FA and FIFA rules that contract must contain all financial terms including your scale of fees. Get the best deal you can for your client and then you will be maximising your own fee anyway. The more they get, the more you get and once you are satisfied you have got the club to push its financial boat out as far as possible then, and only then, start talking about your own fees.

There is, of course, the reverse of that scenario. If you are entitled to charge your client 5% and that equates to £10,000 and the club or employer (other than a football club) offers to pay you £5,000 then why should you not charge the client £5,000? This is not earning at both ends, this is not a double payment. It is merely you receiving the sum to which you were entitled under your contact with the client. As long as the client is clearly told (and as I have said in football there is total transparency now regarding fees, as the client has to sign everything with the club that relates to payments to you) he can hardly complain afterwards. It doesn't mean he won't. Again, the caveat is that in football top-up charges are illegal even apart from the fact that only the player-client can pay when you are acting for the player!

Professional sportsmen have very short memories when it comes to gratitude. I managed to negotiate a contract that provided for a £1m golden balloon payment at the end of the player's contract. All he had to do was stay there. He dumped me because an agent promised to deliver him to another major club. Delivery didn't take place. He did stay where he was and duly got the pay-out. Did he come back to me and say thank you? What do you think? Though I have to say that in his case he did express regret in his autobiography. Bit late, but better late than never.

It is the fact that, generally speaking, you are only as good as your last contract for the player, linked with the ridiculous restriction that a contract can only be for two years, that keeps the agent under constant pressure. I have been fortunate to represent many players who have been extraordinarily loyal. Stand up Chris Waddle, John Harkes, Neil Redfearn, Paul Warhurst, Jonathan Greening, Richard Cresswell, John Oster, Allan Russell, Lee Morris and Craig Beattie as shining examples of that. (Apologies to anybody I might have missed.) But I have to say that these are the exceptions to the rule and very often you will find yourself going to sleep counting the players who you are sure will still be your players when you awake in the morning.

As mentioned, agents' forms are now to be signed by all parties (buying club, selling club and player) and lodged at The FA and in the case of transactions outside The Premiership with The Football League as well, but I wonder just how many players bother to check the fees against the level of charges set out in their contract, although The FA seem to have made a start on doing that for them. I also wonder how many agents say they are acting for a club, get paid and then try to squeeze a bit more from the player, maybe even in cash.

Again, at the time of writing there is some activity on that front. I have been involved, together with most of the leading sports agencies, in establishing The Association of Football Agents (their very own trade union) which will work in close conjunction and co-operation with The FA and is fast becoming recognised as a voice for agents and as a body which will actually take action on agents' behalf as well as acting as in informal information centre. That will involve a considerable amount of self-regulation and only time will tell whether it will cure all of football's ills and root out the rogue agents who do no good, either to the profession or their clients. The problem is that you can only regulate individuals who join the club and the bad guys, who are known to everybody, simply refuse to sign up.

Forgive the cynicism and world-weariness. I have been doing this for many years now.

Playing Contracts – The Practicalities

There is an art to creating a contract and it is necessary to have a template from which to work. Once again, the template is for football but can be adapted easily for other team sports. The terms of the contract used to be easy. If a club were paying a lot of money for a player, then it would want a longish contract, i.e. four to five years or even more. If it wasn't too sure and the player was moving through the internal ranks, then it would give them a year and perhaps try to insert an option for the club to extend the contract on agreed terms if the player proved to be any good.

Much used to be made of signing-on fees. The best agent was the one who got the highest signing-on fee, i.e. the capital sum (which, remember, under the English rules, has to be spread over the period of the contract in equal instalments). Agents like to bump up this figure to the detriment of wages and to their own advantage, particularly because, quite often, they will be on a high percentage of the signing-on fee. In fact, whether you call it signing-on fee, salary or even loyalty payment, it is all part of the same financial package and the player gets it as long as he is at the club at the relevant date. Loyalty payments are more popular with clubs as they don't have to be paid once the player has left the club.

All too often you quote clients a salary figure and they ask what that works out per week. You tell them, adding that they also have a signing-on fee of £X, which, divided by 52, has to be added to their salary. Even though they get the cash-flow advantage of getting that money in advance, they will still find it difficult to get their head around the notion that the capital sum also increases their weekly earnings. Your job, as their agent, is to make it clear to them because, if you accede to their request to go in and ask for a totally unreasonable basic salary, on top of a signing-on fee, then you may not even get past first base with the club.

I have found it to be a fact of footballing life that, more often than not, if you negotiate with a Manager instead of a Chief Executive or a Director, then the Manager will beat a hasty retreat if the initial demands are completely off the wall or are too complicated. They rarely come back with counter-proposals and usually ask you to make your demands first. It is best to try and persuade them to start off by giving you their best shot but that request, more often than not, falls on deaf ears. At Board level, negotiations are generally far more sophisticated. The cut and thrust of offer and counter-offer, give and take, can be quite an exhilarating experience, particularly when you are dealing with a Director or Chief Executive who can actually appreciate some of your more innovative ideas. Having said that, some of the younger managers are learning fast and can be a negotiating match for anybody. What is very unfair (and is certainly not unheard of) is when a club (either through its manager or an official) tries to persuade a player not to use the services of the agent to whom he is contracted (or indeed any agent at all). Having established the licensing system, whatever its failings, the clubs should respect it. And if they don't then they are now breaching The FA Regulations. Mind you, if you complain to The FA you won't win any brownie points and the club will probably not only blacklist you but also the manager will tell all his little pals not to deal with you either. The realities of life in the world of football.

Many clubs are now seeking to dispense with signing-on fees altogether. They are happy to pay a much higher salary so that they know exactly where they stand with their cash-flow. This is likely to prove even more the case when players can terminate their contracts after 60% of what both parties agreed was going to be a five-year term. The current rule is that if a player does not ask for a transfer (i.e. the sale is the club's decision), then he is entitled to be paid up the balance of his signing-on fees. This leads to all sorts of confusion and inevitably to ill feeling. An agent needs to develop goodwill with the clubs and their officials and the last thing you want is to put yourself into a position where a club is going to be wary of ever dealing with you again. Obviously your client's interests must be paramount but, at the same time, you must also not only be seen to be doing the right thing but actually must do the right thing.

Some agents think it clever to manipulate the press. A tabloid will quote from 'an insider source' or someone 'close to the player' that the player is unhappy at their club. The player may deny he ever said it but the seed is sown and the transfer merry-go-round is well and truly on its way. The player's name is in the headlines and, even if the story has not been triggered off because of an illegal approach, then other clubs are immediately alerted to his potential availability. In the current climate, every player has a price and no price is too high for certain clubs. The selling club eventually reluctantly agrees a figure (at the end of the day every agent knows that no club wants to keep a player who does not want to play for them) and then turns around to the player (or, more likely, you, as their agent) and says that it has agreed the price on the basis that it doesn't have to pay the player the balance of his signing-on fees. They may even go further and say that they regard the articles that appeared in the press as tantamount to the player requesting a transfer. Again, technically unsettling a player at his club is a breach of The FA Regulations but I suspect The FA will have enough on their plate trying to administer the rules without worrying about minor breaches like that.

However, the club may well say to you, the player's agent, that it is your job to get suitable compensation from the buying club. This is where all hell breaks loose. An agent may say that his player won't leave unless he gets what is contractually due to him. The club may claim it's not contractually due and anyway what has appeared in the papers was effectively a transfer request. You might go to the buying club and see if it will cough up a bit more money to sweeten the transaction for the player and its response is likely to be that it has sweetened his life sufficiently already with the generous financial package that is on the table. The present club loses its patience and says the deal is off and the player can stay and rot in the reserves (a familiar phrase) or get splinters in his backside from sitting on the subs' bench (equally clichéd). Not a lot of originality in football folk I fear. Just listen to the commentaries and the interviews.

As things stand at present, short of bringing legal action for constructive dismissal, which is an option, albeit an expensive, cumbersome and lengthy one, what can you do? Under the FIFA regulations, there was a concept called 'sporting just cause'. If an established player failed to be selected for 10% of matches in a season, then he did have just cause to terminate his contract and the compensation the club would get would be less than that which they would have received had there been a unilateral breach after the three- (or two-) year period. It's not clear if that option is still available but in any event, it would mean waiting until the end of the season and right now you are the agent of a player caught in the middle of a contractual dispute. Players are notoriously impatient and you would probably get short shrift if you tried to persuade your client to sit it out. I acted for a player whose contract was running down and all he had to do when the contract renegotiations failed to reach the levels to which he aspired, was to sit it out and then sign a pre-contract in the final January of his contract with another club. Did he? Did he heck! He dumped me and then allowed his club to get a fee to enable him to move in the January window under pressure and with the club effectively dictating the terms rather than he himself. So, no, players don't have much patience.

At this point it is quite possible that you are the only person speaking regularly to all parties in the transaction and it is up to you to make the deal happen. If you don't then you lose face with the client – quite possibly lose the client altogether – and you earn nothing from what is likely to have been an expensive and time-consuming episode for you as well.

I always work on the basis that if everybody wants the deal to happen, it generally will. I also believe that if everybody in the transaction gives up a little bit then nobody comes out of it feeling too bruised. So...

The perfect situation is this. You get the buying club to increase the price a bit. You get the selling club to give that uplift to the player as part of the signing-on fee. You get the player to waive some of his signing-on fee as a compromise and also get the buying club to throw something else into the contract. Perhaps a performance-related incentive or a loyalty bonus tucked in at the end of the contract, provided the player is still in the employ of the club at the time and has played a certain number of games. If you can pull all this together with subtle diplomacy, you have earned your fee and the purchase price of this book has been justified.

If it were just a case of term, signing-on fee and basic salary, then anybody could be a football agent. Quite frankly, there appear to be moments when anybody is. Tired of being a second-hand car salesman? Bored with flogging insurance or double-glazing? Had your fill of stocking shelves at the local supermarket? Welcome to the world of football. The fact is, as I have already illustrated by focusing on some of the minutiae of the contract, there is much more to it than that.

The salary should be adjustable, increasing regularly after a number of appearances. If there has been no huge signing-on fee, then perhaps a smaller lump sum after each cluster of appearances may be appropriate. Whether that should be in addition to 'appearance money' is a moot point. The whole concept of appearance money is one that is anathema to anybody outside the world of football. Can you imagine paying your staff an additional sum just for turning up at work? When you think about it, that is what appearance money really is. Players are paid a sum of money to be contracted to the club and they get another sum of money for playing for the club!

Again, as incentive to young players, many clubs are happy to pay ridiculously high appearance monies, whilst giving the player a very low basic salary. If they are doing a man's job by playing in the first team, then they get a man's salary. At the other end of the scale, an older player (or one who has a very poor injury record) may also find himself faced with an incentive-based contract. As the agent, you have to minimise the risks for any client who accepts such a deal. Try to ensure that they get appearance money whether they start or come on as a substitute. In certain circumstances, try and get it for them even when they are just named as part of the first team squad. It may be highly appropriate for a player such as I have just mentioned who is experienced but injury-prone. He shouldn't be penalised if he is fit and available for selection but is just not playing at the manager's whim and fancy. At worst, get a percentage of appearance money for playing as a sub or even as a non-playing sub. What is just about acceptable (and in many clubs is becoming the norm) is 100% when starting, 50% as a playing sub (or 100% if you come on for a whole half or more) and 25% as a non-playing sub. Don't lose sight of the fact that you only get paid on 'guaranteed' income and appearance money is *not* guaranteed.

While taking onboard the potential sporting just cause reason for termination, you still have to look at the contract as it stands at present. If you've been promised the earth but don't play regularly, then to have a break clause in the contract (the right to break only being on the player's part) is very helpful. By this I mean that if the player is fit and doesn't make a certain number of appearances in a year, then he can ask for a transfer to be granted at an agreed fee.

Injuries are always going to be a problem because so many uncertainties in a contract are geared to the player's ability to play. As far as appearance money is concerned, I always feel it is grossly unfair for players to miss out on appearance money just because they have received an injury. So how do you redress that balance?

Well, one way is to say that, provided the injury has been

incurred on club duty (as opposed to the joyriding example I gave before) then the player is entitled to continue to receive appearance money for as many games as he has already played that season. That's a bit of a double-edged sword if he gets injured in his first game. But if he is injured halfway through the season, having been a regular throughout, it means he will continue to get his money for the whole of the rest of the season. To me it seems grossly unreasonable that a player can be financially penalised for being injured by a crunching opposition tackle.

Think of all sorts of bonuses and bring them into your negotiations. The more that are in there, the more likely you are to get something out of it. Success bonuses for winning the League, qualifying for Europe or winning a cup are good even though you may be faced with the club's argument (generally justifiable) that it has a perfectly acceptable squad bonus scheme.

However, if you are representing a superstar, then it is not unreasonable to seek a superbonus. If you are acting for a youngster who is being underpaid on his basic deal, this is a good way of beefing up the package and second-guessing the fact that he may well be breaking into the first team. You can relate his particular bonus to the number of times he actually plays by way of incentivisation. Then there are others such as goal-scoring bonuses for strikers and attacking midfielders, or clean sheet bonuses for keepers and defenders. It's a shame if you are a defensive midfielder, I suppose!

Again, you will meet resistance. The old chestnut of a defence on the part of the club is that football is a team sport and why should it, for example, pay a goalkeeper a bonus when he has made a terrible blunder and a defender comes back to clear off the line?

Loyalty bonuses are not unusual although they don't really have a lot to do with the sort of loyalty that existed between Robin Hood and his Merry Men. Basically, they are a way of getting a player to stay at the club – a bit like golden handcuffs in the business world. If you see through a five-year contract, then you get £100,000, provided you're still there at the end of the period. Make sure the date of payment is the date of the last competitive match of the last season and not the end of the season, otherwise you may have to turn down an exciting offer just to hang on in there for the bonus. Annual loyalty bonuses are not unheard of but, under the present rules, you can't pay a loyalty bonus unless the player has been at the club for at least 12 months.

There are the more personal types of bonuses. The lump sum payment when receiving a first international cap is something to aim for, followed by a further payment on receipt of each further cap. The problem here is the number of internationals and the quality of the opposition, not to mention the quality of the country for which the player is selected. The club may argue, with some justification, that there is no reason why it should pay a player, for example, £10,000, just because he comes on for five minutes in a friendly for Malta against Azerbaijan (no disrespect intended to any Maltese or Azerbaijani readers).

Then, again, they may argue more generally that they shouldn't have to make a substantial payment to a key player only to see him return tired or injured after international duty. It is not unreasonable for the first payment only to be offered for a player starting in a competitive match. Also, it is a fact of life that a player who has qualified to play for England is likely to get a bigger bonus than a player who has qualified to play for, say, Northern Ireland, Wales or even Scotland. (Again, no disrespect intended. I have many friends and players in all those countries. I just report on what actually happens, I don't necessarily instigate the bonus structure!)

If that first competitive match happens to be against Andorra in a World Cup qualifier, so be it. It could just as easily have been France and it is unlikely that any England manager would pick anything but their best side for a competitive tournament qualifier, whatever the opposition may be. However, you may change a whole team in the second half in a friendly and blood someone for just a few minutes. If your player is selected for, say, three consecutive friendlies then it would seem that the manager is already regarding him as part of the squad and there is an argument then that the bonus should be given after the third match.

To override the club's view, that internationals are more of a burden than a benefit, you can say (particularly in the case of a less prestigious team) that the award of a cap to one of its players demonstrates to any player dithering over signing that they have just as much chance of breaking into the England team with the club as they would have if they joined the likes of Manchester United, Arsenal, Liverpool or Chelsea. (I used Newcastle as an example in the last edition but even my loyalty to my team would not stretch to my using them again this time around.) You can also argue that if the team is not doing well but the player still gets international recognition, then the international bonus is a way of compensating him for the paucity of his club bonuses.

While you are at it, see if you can also insert award bonuses, for example, if the player wins the PFA or Football Writers' Player (or Young Player) of the Year Award, or even any European or international awards. Again, they are prestigious for the club even if it is unlikely that your young player will get to that level of achievement. I once put a clause in a contract saying that a player would get a substantial bonus if he scored 20 goals in a promotion year. With one match to go, he was on 17 goals and the team needed to win to get up. He got a hat trick, the club got promotion and everybody was happy. Unlikely, yes; impossible, no. As a lawyer, I would say that I deal with possibilities, not probabilities, and that is also good advice when you are negotiating a sports contract.

Playing Contracts – Cricket

If I seem to be obsessed with football contracts, I make no apology because, certainly in terms of bonuses or incentives, you can apply the principles to most team sports. However, with the 2005 triumph in the Ashes, suddenly cricket became the flavour of the month and there is no doubt that stars such as Andrew Flintoff, Monty Panesar and Kevin Pietersen can be every bit as marketable as leading footballers.

But they will be on central contracts paid by the central body essentially not to play county cricket, and county cricketers are notoriously badly paid so why not try to get extra payments once they have scored a thousand runs and/or taken 50 wickets in a season? The old days of a thousand runs in May or the magic double of a thousand runs and a hundred wickets do seem to be a thing of the past against the background of the present fixture list and I always look to try to get the extraordinary rewarded – the season's fastest century; Man of the Series award; top of the first class averages. There is no doubt that county cricket teams are distinctly more luddite than football clubs but maybe you will be the one to drag them screaming into the twenty-first century.

The whole framework of the cricket contract has changed with the arrival of the England central contract. Test players (and fringe test players) are paid an annual retainer which not only beefs up their annual income but also ensures that their country has first call on their services. It makes for an odd hotchpotch of a season. Whilst the Premier League calls a halt to its fixtures on international weekends, counties just plough straight on, regardless of the fact that a title can stand or fall depending upon the number of players on international duty. It is an oddly vicious circle. You get rewarded by your county for winning matches but then your county wins so many that the spotlight turns on its more successful players who get called into the England team, at which point the weakened county possibly stops winning. So what's the relevance of all that from the agent's point of view?

Well, the real relevance is getting the balance right. The standard England contract leaves no room for negotiation, which means you have to put a lot more effort into the county contract – and, in making that effort, you'll run slap bang into the mass resistance of county committees who are reluctant to change the way they have always done things in the past.

I don't have the space to deal with cricketing – or rugby-playing contracts in as much detail but a few things are worth mentioning. Cricket contracts may well just be for 'the season' rather than the calendar year, leaving the poor old cricketer to make their living the best way they can for the rest of the year. Some counties will pay during pre-season training, i.e. 'the nets', and others won't, so be warned.

It's a precondition of the contract being effective that the cricketer must be registered with the English Cricketing Board (ECB), not necessarily a formality if the cricketer has experienced disciplinary problems in the past, particularly if these were related to illegal substances. Sports contracts are oddities insofar as they are always going to be subject to regulations over which neither employer (club or county) or employee have any control. In the case of cricket, this means that the ECB (the governing body of cricket at home) can change its rules and that change can filter through to the player's contract. The contract clearly says that, 'The cricketer undertakes to read and to abide by the rules, regulations, directives and resolutions of the ECB, the laws of cricket and any International Cricket Council regulations in force from time to time during the currency of this agreement'.

It is not just their domestic body that can change the terms of their employment. The international governing body (the ICC) can as well. Now, as their advisor, there is not a lot you can do about it but you must at least tell them (in writing!). Even if they are not going to read the external rules and regulations that apply to their contract you, at least, should do so. The contract you have so carefully negotiated can change yet again if the rules of the 'club' (i.e. 'the county') change as well, although at least in this case they have to be discussed with the captain of the county and the representatives of the PCA (the Professional Cricketers Association).

However, at all times, the ECB rules take precedence over the club (county) rules. Generally, on the first day of each season, the club or county has to provide the cricketer with its rules for that season.

Quite frankly, the standard cricket contract is so draconian that, in my view, if it were imposed to the letter there is not a court in the civilised world that would enforce it. Torn between his county, the ECB and the ICC and his retainer contract, if he is an international, your client also finds himself obliged to obey the lawful and reasonable directions of the captain (or deputy captain) of any club or side for which he may be selected to play. Even though he has just signed up as a player, he has to provide coaching services if asked and, although he may only be employed for the season, he can't, without the club's consent, accept other employment on his own account or carry on any business, calling or profession (shades of the football contract there, but at least generally footballers earn enough money to compensate).

The contract generously states that the club's consent is not to be withheld 'when in the reasonable opinion of the club, the proper performance by the cricketer and their obligations under this agreement is not affected' (fair enough?) 'or the interests of the club are not harmed'. That seems to me to be too wide and potentially dangerous.

Let's say a cricket county is sponsored by insurance company X and you, the agent, negotiate a contract with insurance company Y for your player to endorse Y's products. X complains and the county says that its interests are being harmed. Hardly fair, but at least you must have a catch-all clause in the endorsement contract stating that the player won't be in breach of the contract if he is stopped by his county from performing the same. The whole concept of ensuring 'no breach arising from the implementation of the club contract' is one I will examine in more detail in the chapter concerning commercial contracts.

One interesting point is that the player must 'work every day including Sunday and Bank Holidays and during such hours the club shall reasonably require and not take any holiday'. Again, not unreasonable, you might say, but the Working Time Regulations in the United Kingdom stipulate that an employee shall not work more than 48 hours per week and with travelling, playing and training time it seems to me there is every chance that the statute is being regularly breached.

And finally there is an odd club/county clause which says that your player must 'ensure that any sponsorship, advertising or similar promotional activity undertaken by him will not prevent him, in the event of him being selected for any England representative team, from complying with the requirements of any sponsorship, advertising or similar promotional activity associated with playing for any such team'.

This sort of clause makes our job much more difficult. How on earth is the agent supposed to know what might be the requirements of any England sponsor when they don't know when their client might be selected for England and certainly can only hazard a guess as to who might be the England sponsor at the time? You are juggling all these balls in the air – county, country, sponsor, county sponsor, country sponsor – and if you take your eye off any of them, then they could all come crashing to the ground and, with them, any confidence your client may have in your ability to steer him through without any of the balls hitting him on the head. And, believe me, cricket balls really hurt!

Representation of Team / League Sport Athletes versus Representation of Athletes in 'Individual' Sports

When an agent represents an athlete in a team/league sport, the agent's primary responsibilities involve negotiating the relationship between the athlete and the team and then handling various business issues on behalf of the athlete. These may include sponsorship agreements, charitable activities including launching an athlete foundation, website development, camps and, if the agent is an attorney, legal issues. In addition if the agent is a licensed investment advisor he may well be expected to advise about how to handle the athlete's earnings.

The team and league take care of many other issues for the athlete. For example, the athlete's competition schedule is automatically the schedule assigned to the team by the league and any other organisations or competitions in which the team competes. The team handles transportation for the player to training camps and games, as well as all accommodations on the road – hotels, meals (or provides meal money), support for dealing with the media and fans, and so on. The team should also provide professional trainers and medical personnel to assist the player with ailments and injuries. The team will have a public information staff to deal with the media and many other enquiries directed to the player. The team and the league may even help field, arrange, and organise charitable and community appearances by the player (which he may or may not be required to do under the terms of his contract with the team). The team provides training facilities and coaches who are supposed to be responsible for guiding the player's improvement on the field. The team may also have personnel to help the athlete with other needs – securing housing, hiring domestic help, responding to fan mail, and a host of other local services which may even include serving as a concierge for the athlete – securing tickets, dinner reservations, and anything else the athlete may need. In most situations, the player's agent will only be called upon to perform services not performed by the team. So far, I suspect, none of this is very different from what happens in the UK.

The world of individual sports is very different. Take tennis as an example. The ATP Tour (for men) and WTA Tour (for women) provide a schedule of events, but the player (in conjunction with his or her agent) must decide which of these events (as well as which exhibition events and Grand Slam tournaments – the French, US, and Australian Opens and Wimbledon) to enter. The player is responsible for travel arrangements, but there may be a 'players hotel' at events. The player must hire his (and please take it for granted I also mean 'her') own coach and arrange for facilities to practise. There may be trainers provided by the circuit at events, but the player is generally responsible for his own medical and training services on a day-to-day basis. At events there should be an event staff to deal with the media on-site, but the player and his agent will generally be responsible for fielding calls and enquiries from the media and for arranging any community or charitable appearances by the player.

As a result, there are many additional services a sports agent (or sports management company) can provide to an individual sports athlete. The agent can be called upon to select a coach or at least to negotiate the employment (or independent contractor) agreement between the coach and the player and to handle disputes between the player and the coach. Sports agents in individual sports are often former players and may themselves provide scouting or coaching services. For example, the agent may tell a young tennis player the best strategy for defeating a veteran player in an upcoming match. The agent will field media enquiries and requests for autographs, auction items for charities, appearance invitations, and various other requests from charitable and community organisations, as well as general fan mail to the player, and may maintain the player's calendar. The player may want the agent to serve as a travel agent or as an intermediary between the athlete and a travel agency, arranging for all transportation and hotel accommodations for the player. The agent (or his assistant) may become a *de facto* assistant/concierge for the individual sports athlete, and can handle everything from opening bank accounts and registering cars to arranging for and supervising domestic help and home repair folks to taking clothes to and from the dry cleaners.

The Player Agent
in the United States

by Mark Levinstein

In the United States, the rules and restrictions an agent must follow depend on the particular sport and the competitive level of the athlete, the age and education level of the athlete, the state where the athlete lives or is located (or where the athlete will compete), and the particular services the agent will provide to the athlete. It is not possible for a book of this length to provide you with everything you need to know about the relevant rules and regulations, but we can identify the categories and provide you with a basic understanding.

Over the past 30 years, as the sports agent has emerged as an important position in the sports industry in the United States, there have been public calls for legislation and regulation to govern the athlete representation process. Sports agents have been criticized for (1) mismanaging athlete income, (2) charging athletes excessive fees, (3) engaging in undisclosed conflicts of interest, (4) representing athletes in an incompetent manner, (5) causing student athletes to receive prohibited funds or otherwise eliminating their eligibility to compete in amateur or collegiate sports (and thereby damaging the institutions that benefit from the athletes' services), and (6) misappropriating athletes' funds. As a result of vociferous calls for legislation and regulations, the major sports players associations, the federal government, a number of state governments, and the National Collegiate Athletic Association (NCAA) have attempted to promulgate rules or laws governing agent relationships with athletes.

Certification as an Agent by the Players Associations of the Four Major Professional Sports Leagues in the United States:

As a first matter, the four major United States sports leagues are Major League Baseball (MLB), the National Basketball Association (NBA), the National Football League (NFL), and the National Hockey League (NHL). I realize the UK reader may find it hard to accept and understand that Major League Soccer (MLS) is not in the top four.

The players in each of these sports are represented by a labor union, or players' association, each of which is recognized as the exclusive collective bargaining representative of the players under the federal labor laws of the United States. All four of these players' associations (the MLB Players Association [MLBPA], the NFL Players Association [NFLPA], the National Basketball Players Association [NBPA], and NHL Players Association [NHLPA]) have negotiated overall agreements with their respective leagues that virtually govern all terms and conditions of employment, but generally give players some freedom to negotiate their individual salaries. Players are assigned to teams based on an initial draft, in which the worst teams from the previous season are given the right to make the first selections in the first round of the draft before the next season. The collective bargaining agreements may specify minimum player salaries for players, including higher minimum salaries for players with more years of experience in the league. The collective bargaining agreements in the NFL, NBA, and NHL contain 'salary caps', placing absolute limits on the maximum total amounts teams in those leagues can pay all the players on their teams. In some of these leagues there are also limits on the amount a team can pay any player in a single year and certain leagues have rookie salary limits or 'rookie caps', which limit the salary that can be paid to a player in his first season, and the rookie cap for a particular player may depend on how soon that player was picked in the draft (higher rookie cap for the first draft pick of the year, less for the second draft pick, and so on).

Under United States labour laws, because the players' associations and leagues could negotiate all the terms and conditions of the players' employment, the law permits the players' associations and leagues to agree that the players' associations have effectively delegated the right to negotiate player salaries (within the limits of the various minimum salaries and salary caps) to players and to agents who represent the players. Under this fiction, that the agents are working for the players' association when they negotiate individual player salaries, the MLBPA, NBPA, NFLPA, and NHLPA have all entered into collective bargaining agreements with their respective leagues that only permit teams in those leagues to negotiate with agents who have been certified by the respective players' associations. Therefore, unless and until an agent has been certified by the NFLPA, no NFL team will negotiate with that agent and any agreement reached by a team with that agent would not be enforceable by the team. The same is true with the other three leagues and their respective players' associations.

To be certified by one of the players' associations to represent players in that league, an agent must comply with their regulations, apply for certification, attend mandatory agent education programmes, pass certain certification tests, and pay annual fees. Some of the players' associations specify maximum amounts player agents can charge players for representing them in contract negotiations, give players the absolute right to terminate a player agent on very short notice (e.g. 14 days), mandate the form of agreement between players and their agents, and specify that all disputes between players and their agents must be decided in arbitration conducted under rules and procedures specified by the players' association. To get information about the regulations governing agents (which the NFLPA calls 'contract advisors') representing players in the National Football League, obtain an NFLPA 'Application for Certification', and find other information relating to the NFLPA and representing professional football players, you

can go via the Internet to www.nflpa.org/Agents/main.asp For
the NHLPA the same information is available at www.nhlpa.
com/Agents/ In Major League Baseball, after an MLB player
retains an agent, if that agent has not yet been certified by
the MLBPA, he or she must contact the MLBPA in New York
City ((212) 826-0808) for the MLBPA agent regulations and
further information about becoming certified. An application
to become an NBA player agent and the regulations governing
NBA player agents can be found at www.nbpa.com/agentapp.
php

State Agent Legislation:

Of course, agents are also bound by the restrictions imposed
both by State Agent and Federal Agent Legislation.

Federal Agent Legislation:

The NCCA: The National Collegiate Athletic Association
(NCAA) is an organization of all the major colleges and
universities in the United States. NCAA athletes are not paid for
their services, but they may be eligible for athletic scholarships
and financial aid. To be admitted to a college or university and
to be eligible to play on an NCAA sport team or in an NCAA
competition, student athletes must meet certain minimum
academic eligibility requirements. Then, after they enroll at
an NCAA college or university, to remain eligible to compete,
athletes must be enrolled in school and working toward a
degree and must maintain a minimum grade point average.
To maintain this system of 'student athletes' competing
without being paid, the NCAA has strict rules and regulations
prohibiting the payment of athletes, whether payment is in
money, products, or services and whether payment is directly
to the athlete or to his family or friends. If an athlete signs
with an agent it is likely to terminate his eligibility to continue
to participate in NCAA competitions. Therefore, the schools
that benefit from the student athlete's services see agents

as individuals who can severely damage a school's athletic programmes by causing athletes to leave the college ranks for a professional career. An agent who is perceived as causing a player to go pro before the player is ready and thereby damaging the athlete and the school the athlete deserted is likely to be perceived as a pariah, making it much more difficult for the agent to find athlete clients in the future.

In some cases, athletes have signed agent contracts or have taken money and have continued to play in NCAA competitions on behalf of their schools. After their ineligibility has been discovered, the schools for which they played have generally been required to forfeit all competitions in which the ineligible athlete competed, and there have at times been other sanctions as well. Forfeiture of competitions often means the school will be required to return financial awards associated with those competitions, which may cost the school millions of dollars. Sanctions can include exclusion from various season-ending competitions or exclusion from having the school's games televised, other penalties that can cost an educational institution millions of dollars while also damaging the school's future recruitment of athletes.

In addition, several states turned to their state legislators in an effort to protect their colleges and universities (especially major state-owned institutions) from the loss of the services of top athletes. The states were also seeking someone to prosecute if an athlete's undisclosed ineligibility causes a state school to forfeit payments associated with a competition. As a result, certain states have passed legislation making it a criminal offence for an agent to sign an agency contract with a college-eligible athlete in those states, without first providing the affected college or university with notice of the intention to do so and giving the school a period of time to (a) try to talk the athlete out of signing the contract, and (b) ensure that the athlete does not play after the athlete has become ineligible.

Agents Providing Specific Services to Athletes:

If an agent is providing legal services to an athlete in the United States, the agent's actions will be governed by the laws and rules governing attorneys in each of the states where the agent practises law. Those state laws and regulations prescribe standards of conduct for licensed attorneys concerning, among other things, full disclosure to clients, solicitation of clients, advertising, fees, minimum competency and conflicts of interest. Difficult questions are presented by the sports agent/attorney who provides a variety of services to his or her clients. For example, a sports agent/attorney may provide advice about contracts with teams, events, and sponsors, provide tax advice, prepare tax returns, advise about the purchase of real estate and various other purchases or investments, draft prenuptial agreements and wills, and advise the athlete about a host of other issues. If an agent is not a licensed attorney, the fact must be openly and prominently disclosed to the athlete and the agent should avoid providing advice about any subject that clearly involves the practice of law in the United States.

If the agent provides any advice in the United States or to a United States athlete about financial issues or investments, there are a myriad of state and federal regulations that will govern that relationship, including substantial civil and criminal penalties for individuals providing those services improperly and/or without complying with various certification and regulatory requirements.

As in the UK, very often the agent is the man everybody loves to hate, the man who ultimately takes the blame for his client's shortcomings. The object of the exercise is maximization of income and profile whilst, whenever necessary, also maximizing damage limitation. Not every agent has a lifestyle as glamorous or dangerous as that of author Harlan Coben's hero, Myron Bolitar, but if you play it right it can be a career unlike any other and a rewarding one at that.

Playing Contracts – Rugby

As with the Ashes victory, success in the Rugby World Cup also reinvented the commercial opportunities for those who partook in the sport. Before then Rugby had been in a state of conflict and flux for some years. Having been 'shamateur' for such a long time, professional rugby inevitably brought with it the chance for new-found wealth that had been around for so long in the worlds of golf, tennis, boxing and football. Whilst TV money wasn't as generous as that available to football, it was still there and suddenly rugby found itself faced with players and their agents demanding contracts of six figures a year. But old habits still died hard and rugby continued to be supported better at international than club level. So the clubs decided quite simply that if their players were selected for international duty, then they wouldn't pay them. However, the clubs still wanted to have their cake and eat it, and they retained their rights to enforce the club contract even when players were off playing for their country. They do, however, acknowledge that players may have different promotional obligations when on international duty and that these may well conflict with their club obligations. Again, at the time of writing the World Cup victory seems to have been forgotten as the sport once again does its best to tear itself apart. Inevitable, I suppose, as that seems to be the object of the game on the pitch as well. As you can probably tell I don't like rugby. I think it should get done under the Trades Description Act. Rugby Football? I thought a ball had to be round and not a thing that was melon shaped and covered in leather!

Anyway, I do have to assume that some readers of this book will have clients who do play rugby so, how does all this affect you? I think you have to accept that in the real world you have far less chance of substantial renegotiation of cricket and rugby contracts than you do with a football club, which in a way puts an even greater responsibility on you to make sure your client fully understands what he is saddled with rather than what you have done for him. Of course, you may get him £10,000 a year more than he would have got for himself but you will still find that he has had to give away all of his personal image rights. A typical rugby contract has a schedule attached which is headed 'licensing rights and promotional services' and the standard opening clause simply states, 'The player grants the club the irrevocable and exclusive right to use and exploit the licensing rights (with the power to grant sub-licences)…'

Once again there are an enormous number of pitfalls for the unwary, contained in such a few words. In the first place, any grant of rights should be limited 'for the duration of this agreement only'. The last thing you want is for the club to be able to continue to exploit your client's image once he has moved on to another club or even retired with celebrity status. Again, you should try and seek some control over the grant of sub-licences. If your player suddenly becomes a superstar at international level, that will flow down into his club profile. Your client is not going to thank you if he has to stand idly by whilst the club happily sub-licences his image to one commercial sponsor after another, for their own benefit and without the player receiving any material rewards. The way around it is to say that no sub-licences can be granted without the player's consent and, at worst, you can add the words, 'such consent not to be unreasonably withheld'.

Further, you can try for a benchmark of income share and here 50% might be appropriate. You have to try and retain some control over your client's image, particularly as the standard contract goes on to say 'The Player hereby appoints the Club to be his attorney and in his name and on his behalf to do all such acts and things and to execute all deeds and documents and in his name and on his behalf to exercise all powers... to prevent any infringement of the Licensing Rights by any person'.

Just to demonstrate the balance of power between club and player, it is worth looking at Clause 3 of the schedule:

> For the avoidance of doubt:
>
> (b) The player will not himself use or exploit the Licensing Rights nor licence any third party to use or exploit the Licensing Rights other than with the prior consent of the Club which it may in its absolute discretion withhold;
>
> (c) save to the extent that such agreement or use or exploitation would result in a breach of any other provision of this Agreement the Player remains free to enter into any sponsorship, endorsement or promotional agreement and to use and exploit his name, likeness, image, voice and biographical details in any medium other than in his capacity as a Player for the Club;
>
> (d) the licence granted by the Player under paragraph 1 above will survive the termination of this Agreement;
>
> (e) the Licensing Rights do not include any right to use or exploit the name or likeness of the Player in his capacity as a member of any international rugby football team.

As well as the crumb that is tossed back to the player pursuant to Clause 4:

> In order to assist the Player to comply with the obligations under paragraph 3 above the Club hereby agrees, as soon as reasonably practicable, throughout the period of Employment to notify the Player of all sponsorship, advertising or similar promotional arrangements relating to the Player in his capacity as a Player for the Club, entered into by the Club.

But what they give with one hand, they snatch back with the other as is evident from Clause 5:

All intellectual property rights in or arising out of any use or exploitation of the Licensing Rights by the Club or its sub-licencees or assignees and/or the provision by the Player of the Promotional Services will (as between the Player and the Club) be and remain the exclusive property of the Club or its assignees, as the case may be.

As if there is anything left for you to market, the club has a final whammy in Clause 6(a):

The Club reserves the right to require that the Player will, during the Employment, (save where such requirement shall be in breach of the terms or in conflict with any pre-existing contract entered into with the Player permitted by this Agreement):

wear any relevant items of clothing and use any relevant items of Playing Kit and Leisurewear supplied to him by the Club on and off the field when providing the Promotional Services, playing as a member of the Club, during training and at Club practices, when on Club trips and when involved in any other way with the Club as required by the Club.

Clause 6(b) is also tricky as it says your player can't 'wear, carry on or display Playing Kit or Leisurewear bearing a visible logo or brand without the prior consent of the Club'. That means that, if the player is given a kit bag by a sportswear manufacturer, he can't even carry his stuff around in it without the consent of the club. It doesn't take a genius to work out that this is going to make your job virtually impossible when it comes to getting sponsorship opportunities from sportswear companies.

The problem is that it is all very well negotiating a fresh contract for an established international star and using his pulling power and playing ability to refuse to accept those onerous restrictions. The club may well want him so badly that it'll give in on everything.

But what if you are acting for a talented youngster who is

all potential? The club uses its clout and insists on its standard restriction. Your client becomes visibly successful and the club is in the driving seat when it comes to cashing in on his talent. Your client as a youngster will be only too keen to sign whatever is stuck in front of him (this is the same in every sport) and may even regard your interference as unwelcome. The best you can hope for is to ensure that the contract is either to be renegotiated if your player gets a certain number of international caps or that the licensing restrictions are varied at that point.

One particular issue in rugby is the question of injury as the chances are much greater than in most sports. Rugby clubs are like most employers insofar as they want to pay as little as possible to an employee who can't do his work. The fact that his inability to do the job has arisen as a result of an injury sustained within the remit of the job description doesn't appear to be particularly relevant!

Your client breaks his neck in a scrum (or whatever happens in a scrum – I have to confess that not only is rugby not my favourite sport but I've never watched a match all the way through, having been distracted by paint drying and flies crawling up and down window panes) and the club immediately turns to Clause 4.3 of the standard Rugby Football Union contract which states:

> If the Player shall at any time during the Employment be prevented by illness, injury or accident from playing Rugby or training for the Club (which shall mean being able to participate in full-contact training and being fit for selection to play) or from carrying out non-playing/training duties during the close season for an aggregate of 8 weeks in any 12 calendar months or an aggregate period of 13 weeks during the Term (in calculating which the Club shall be entitled to take into account any period of unavailability under a different contract of employment with the Club during the twelve months preceding the commencement of the Employment) then the Club shall thereafter be entitled (but not obliged) to terminate this

Agreement by giving not less than four weeks' written notice to the Player provided that at the time of giving such notice:

(a) the Player shall still be unable to play Rugby or train for the Club; and

(b) the Club shall have received from a qualified medical practitioner instructed by the Club and with whom the Player shall co-operate a certificate dated not earlier than ten days before the date on which the said notice is given stating that in the opinion of such medical practitioner the Player will be unfit for a period of 10 days from the date of the medical practitioner's inspection to play Rugby.

Clause 4.4 gets worse as this says that if the player is

(a) not selected to play for the Club's First XV at all in any one Season during the currency of this Agreement; or

(b) fails to attain and/or maintain the level of fitness required (from time to time) in accordance with Schedule 3 within a period of 14 days after written notice requiring him to do so; or

(c) continues to fail to train and/or be available to play for the Club seven days after written notice requiring him to do so;

The Club may at its sole discretion at any time thereafter terminate this Agreement by giving not less than one week's written notice to the Player.

So what can you do about it? Well, you can try to exclude any injury period arising from a playing or training injury (very much as I tried to explain in varying Clause 8 of the Premier League contract), or you can try to get the aggregate period extended and the window period reduced.

If the club won't agree to that, then try to squeeze a contribution to insurance from it and if it is being really mean, then at least make sure you put in writing to your client the advice that he should be taking out insurance himself. Either put him in touch with a broker or get some quotes on his behalf. You can do no more. At the end of the day, sports clients are led with difficulty to the well but generally still prefer to drink champagne.

Commercial Contracts

If you have followed my advice you will find that you are the agent for your clients, not only in respect of their on-the-pitch contracts, but also in respect of their off-the-pitch (and hopefully remunerative) commercial activities. I mentioned earlier that the first piece of wisdom to drum into a client's head is that if he doesn't perform on the pitch or on the field or in the ring or in the saddle, or even at the table in the case of a snooker player, then you won't be able to perform for him off the pitch, out of the ring, away from the table, etc.

A sportsperson's career is a fragile thing and our media delight in taking away what they have given. There is a special department in Fleet Street responsible for manufacturing feet of clay.

But, for the sake of this book (and your bank balance), let's imagine that you have managed to get hold of a hot property. They have either scored a winning goal in a World Cup Final, won a Test Series single-handed, broken the tries record for their country, led them to the Triple Crown, grabbed a Gold medal against all the odds at the Olympics or simply touched the heart of the nation by being a gallant loser. Whichever it may be, the fact of the matter is that before the ink is dried on the next day's tabloids, your phone has started to ring and the roller coaster sets off on its upwards ride.

I once spoke at a conference and used the title 'Making the Talent Spin Gold' and that's about as accurate as it gets.

There are thousands of potential sponsors out there willing to sprinkle the gold dust and it's a question of how far you can get the heap to rise before it topples over.

There are a few things you have to establish with your client at the point of take-off. How far do they want to go? There are some people out there who take to fame like ducks to water. It is all fun and continues to be so however many times they sign an autograph, speak to the cameras or endorse a product. Then there are the others who love it at first but quickly grow to hate the loss of privacy. The money is nice but what about the ability to draw the curtains on your life from time to time? And, finally, there are the shy and unassuming superstars for whom every public appearance outside the sporting arena is agony. Like fish out of water, they can only die and it's your duty to support them, not kill them off just for the sake of a few quick bucks.

There are innumerable ways of making money for a successful client whose face and name have become part of the lives of millions of householders. This volume concentrates on the common ones. The first onslaught is likely to come from the media. Now, the one sure way to upset our friendly little scribes and fill their pens with poison is to refuse to speak to them unless you are paid for it. On the other hand, you can get good money for in-depth interviews or regular columns and those paying for them are not going to be overjoyed if their competitors get as much access to your client without paying for it.

You can deal with the problem in several ways. With the wonderful world of technology you can set up a website for your client, make sure it is kept up to date and let the press, as a whole, know that it is there. Websites themselves are a good way of making money provided they are regularly updated, professionally set up and provide interesting information. Sponsors can be persuaded to advertise on them or have them linked to their own sites. Items can be auctioned online or competitions organised. There are several reputable companies out there running websites for athletes and, unless you have specific IT knowledge yourself, my view is that it's safer to do a deal with one of them. If you are not going down the website route, you can issue regular press releases or hold press conferences when there is something important to discuss. However, always make sure that what is asked or answered is relatively bland. The good stuff you save for whoever has a contract with you and provided you (and your client – always a bit more difficult to control) keep the balance, everybody is fairly happy.

There are certain set phrases you will need to insert in a contract with a newspaper publisher. The payment and the number of interviews may be obvious but what constitutes an interview needs to be carefully defined. Also, the limits of the interview have to be set out. Particularly as far as the tabloids are concerned, sport is a very separate category from news, entertainment, gossip and scandal. You don't want to commit your client to 12 interviews a year and find that 3 of them are required by the paper in relation to three different girlfriends with whom he may have had relationships in the relevant period. In a perfect world, you want to limit the interviews to his particular sport and whilst you might want to give your 'favoured' paper an option on non-sporting stories, you do leave yourself wide open to attacks from rival papers if they've absolutely no chance of getting an exclusive.

Make sure there are special provisions for one-off situations. For example, a transfer in football, a change of county or club in cricket or rugby, a classics winner in racing, a World Championship in snooker or boxing or an Olympic gold medal in athletics. Also, try to get your choice of journalists to conduct the interviews. Just as there are good and bad agents, there are also good and very bad journalists. My policy is to give every journalist one chance and one chance only. As soon as the confidence is breached or an off-the-record comment is reported, then they have to go on your blacklist. You simply can't afford to take chances as breaches of confidentiality can only reflect badly on both you and your client.

Always get copy control for every article. Headline and photographic control are equally important because a misleading headline can turn an innocuous interview into something quite different. It is simply not worthwhile having your client suspended for bringing their particular sport into disrepute just for the sake of a few pieces of silver. Never lose sight of the fact that their sporting activities are paramount.

One clause which is desirable is for the paper, to which your client is exclusively contracted, to be obliged to tell you in advance when they are planning to run a non-sporting story about them and to give you a right of reply. If you are contracted to the *Daily Gossip*, then the likelihood is that the *Gossip* will be the first to receive a phone call if your client is seen rolling out of a nightclub at 4 o'clock, dead drunk, with a couple of girls of dubious reputation hanging on his arm.

Try to look for an indemnity in respect of any article, although there is less justification for that when you have copy control. If the article has been sent through to your office and you have failed to pick up something relevant, then you have to carry the can as far as your client is concerned. However, if they slip something back in that causes grief or if they have just gone ahead with a 'publish and be damned' attitude, then apart from any damages, you should have the right to terminate whilst at the same time being entitled to be paid up to the value of the entire balance of the contract.

It is a balancing act to ensure that not too much is given away, while you retain the right to give other trivial interviews which say little but are good for public relations. You'll just have to live with the fact that the tabloids will take a two-line interview, add old stuff to it so it fills the page and then slap 'World Exclusive' on it. Don't even think about applying to the Press Complaints Commission. They are toothless and, in my opinion, a complete waste of space. By making the complaint you give up any rights you may have to pursue the offender through the courts and, whilst defamation actions are dangerous and expensive, there are times when it may well be worth the effort if you are absolutely sure of your ground. Never sue for a matter of principle but if there is a real chance of recovering substantial damages, then there are times when such an action is the only course of action when you are confronted by a vindictive reporter. Don't be scared off by the editor saying that the journalist sticks to their story or the Legal Department claiming 'witnesses'. If you are sure of your ground (and sometimes with sports personalities you have to be very sure of your ground), then go for it but first conduct a cross-examination along the lines of the Spanish Inquisition of your client. Once you actually start litigation it is very difficult to stop.

Never give away too much. If a paper wants to use your client in an advertising campaign or to promote another unrelated product offer, then that must be a matter for separate negotiation. They may be giving away cans of Pepsi whilst you have a deal with Coke. Give them free rein to do what they want and you and your client may find yourselves on the wrong end of litigation.

Ensure that there is a cross-reference to your client's playing contract and that his obligations to his club, federation or sport are the top priorities. In the case of any conflict, then the playing contract must take precedence. That gets you out of a situation where the manager calls your client in for extra training on an afternoon when his contractual newspaper has set up a major photographic shoot. They may have incurred substantial costs but they won't be able to load them onto you if you are postponing or cancelling for a good cause.

Always be on the lookout for marketing opportunities that can swell the value of what is already, hopefully, a valuable contract. Try and get a commitment to joint promotions for the likes of posters, T-shirts, calendars or whatever other products your client may be about to endorse.

There may now be a very good reason to 'incorporate' your client before the value of their name starts to spiral. I touched upon this briefly in earlier chapters but let us take the case of little Tommy Tucker who has become an icon straight after an England World Cup success. He has the nickname 'Tucko'. What you can do (with the help of a solicitor and an accountant) is form Tommy Tucker Promotions Limited.

Tucko enters into an agreement with that company to give them all his future promotional rights. (Try and limit those to the UK as there may well be a good tax reason to set up an offshore company, for their foreign rights, if he goes to play abroad and thus becomes non-resident.)

It may be that he wants his partner or mum to run a fan club and they can be employed by the company to do just that and they will enter into a service agreement to provide their services to Tommy Tucker Promotions Limited in respect of any contract they may have entered into. TTP Limited will then register 'Tucko' as a trademark because it is a 'sign capable of being represented graphically, which is capable of distinguishing goods or services of one undertaking from those of another undertaking'. The Trademark Act 1994, widened the scope of things you could protect to include words – including personal names – although a signature has always been capable of registration.

The problem you have is that, without a crystal ball, it's hard to second-guess the various use classes in which the name must be registered. Registering the name in relation to clothing does not give protection to printed material like calendars. Protecting the name on mugs doesn't help with curtains and carpets. Once again, the responsibility for the balancing act will fall on you, but then that is why you get your commission.

Television and Commercials

From media interviews it is a huge jump to TV programmes and commercials but, in terms of revenue, it is certainly worth making the effort. You have to be realistic and accept that no advertising agency is going to approach you to use your client in a television advertisement unless your client has become instantly recognisable. Similarly, no television or production company is going to make a programme about them or feature them in a programme or documentary unless there is a peg of particular interest upon which they can hang their hat. Once again, whilst you can't do it for your client in their particular sport, you can work upon what your client gives you with their sporting achievements. Being an agent is as much about spin as being a politician.

Anyway, let's assume your client has handed it all to you on a plate. For example, they have scored the winning goal in a World Cup Final, they have won the 100 metres at the Olympic Games, they have brought a Wimbledon singles title home to England or they have captured the undisputed heavyweight title of the world. The odds are very long that you will represent a client who will do any of those things but you not only have to dream, you have to be ready when those dreams come true. And be sure that you're agreement does permit you to continue to represent him when his playing days are over or else you may miss out on a successful media career. Just look at what the likes of Gary Lineker, Andy Gray, Chris Waddle, Alan Shearer, Alan Hansen, Mike Atherton and Sir Ian Botham have achieved in broadcasting.

Whichever of the above your client has achieved, the phone doesn't stop ringing in your office and you finally agree, in principle, to him filming a TV advertisement, in order to promote a particular product. Now the first thing you have to accept is that this will effectively stop your client from promoting any competitive products in the immediate future, so it has to be financially attractive. Before you get him to sign anything, you must also check his existing commercial contracts to ensure that the advertisement won't put him in breach of any of those. If your client is sponsored by a footwear company and that sponsorship contract also includes leisurewear, you are going to have to think twice before agreeing to appear in an advertisement for leisure clothing, even if that company doesn't manufacture sporting goods.

The merchandising contracts are to be explained shortly but this is just laying down the marker – they have to be drafted very carefully and you must ensure that you don't give away too much too early for too little money. It's all very well delighting your client by telling him you got him half a dozen pairs of boots a year but he won't be so pleased when you have to tell him that the very same contract means that you have to turn down a six-figure sum that is on offer to advertise polo shirts.

Assuming you have set up the service company for your client, it is very likely that he, personally, will be asked to sign an 'inducement letter'. This confirms that the company has been induced to enter the contract by him and he will, in effect, personally guarantee the due performance of the contract by way of the provision of his services.

If the agreement is for a commercial, make sure you see the script and always ask where the advertisement is to be shown and on how many occasions. If it is just going to be aired on non-terrestrial television, the fee will be less than for terrestrial and non-terrestrial. Check to see if there is to be a tie-in poster campaign on buses, trains and roadside sites. Again, that will push up the price. The advertising agency may well offer a 'buy-out'. That means your client gets just one payment and they can use the advertisement as often as they like, wherever they like. Depending on how much faith you have in your client, you may be better off giving them limited rights and an option for further 'bursts' (i.e. showings) of the advertisement, where they pay more money depending upon the number of times they show it and where.

Insert a time limit on the initial period of exploitation; say six months. Make sure they keep to the script you have approved and always try to get in a clause that says there can't be any substantial changes to it without your consent. Tie them down to a shooting time. They will always ask for more than they need so stand your ground when they say it is impossible to complete the filming in the time you have offered them.

I have already stressed that you need a non-culpable get-out clause in case your client's sporting employer flexes its muscles and says he can't attend the filming. The advertising agency probably wants to be able to use stills from the advertisement to promote the campaign but limit that carefully. Again, if they want to use stills at points of sale, they should be prepared to pay for that.

It goes without saying that if there is an overnight stop or a distance to travel then accommodation and transportation should be first class. Don't lose the plot and always ensure that if there is any overnight stop, your client can be able to report for training, fresh as a daisy, the following day. Nothing is calculated to upset a coach or manager more than to have one of their players turn up knackered after pursuing his private commercial interests.

It may be that your client becomes so famous that a production company or a TV network wants to make a programme about him. Copy control is absolutely essential as it is inevitable that both the director and the production crew will get close to your client over the extended period of filming and, at some stage, they will drop their guard. Look what happened to poor old Graham Taylor. If a programme like this does get made, you have to think about sell-through videos and Internet publications which may be spin-offs from the programme.

Don't lose out on any potential income from those or anything else. The programme may well be licensed to other countries throughout the world and the appropriate wording to ensure that your client shares in everything is to refer to 'gross receipts (to include monies or monies' worth) received by the Company and attributable to or arising from the exploitation of the programme'. You need to place an obligation on the company to take all necessary actions to recover receivables and, whilst they will want your client's share to be based on net receipts, you will want to set out carefully what expenses can and can't be deducted. Always keep an eye open for the possibility of a tie-in book. You certainly do *not* want to give away all the rights for that, as it may be more valuable than the programme or the series itself.

Accounting obligations are important, of course, as you will see when I look at a specific licensing deal but meanwhile, in relation to programmes of this nature, you are probably looking at accounts being produced twice a year with monies being remitted 60 to 90 days thereafter. That's the way the industry generally works and they are unlikely to change their practices for you or your client.

The company will want a 'lock-out', i.e. it won't want your client to take part in any other programmes or give any major interviews within an agreed time framework, particularly if they are going to be paying the sort of money I am confident you will be able to achieve for your client.

Licences and Endorsements

If you take all the proper steps along the way then, by the time your client is at the peak of his earning power, he and his image will be carefully protected properties, the rights to which you will be able to licence through to different companies for all sorts of products and concepts.

Let's take a typical scenario of a manufacturer who has a particular product that they think is suitable to market in conjunction with your client's name. This may or may not be a sporting product. It can just as easily be a child's lunchbox as a mini football. So let's think about the lunchbox.

The agreement will be between your client's promotion company and the manufacturer. Set out clearly what the manufacturer does and how they want to use the intellectual property belonging to your client. The manufacturer, for their part, will want confirmation that the company has got the exclusive rights to your client's services.

Set out the definitions to be contained in the licence carefully. The territory needs to be narrowly defined. You may only want to give the right for the product to be manufactured in the United Kingdom and the Republic of Ireland. The manufacturer might want the whole of Europe or even the whole world, and how much you grant them in turn will depend on the amount of money that you charge. The use of the Internet as a selling vehicle has substantially moved the goalposts as far as territories are concerned. If your licensee is based in the UK but offers products for sale on its website which are purchased in South America, then it will require 'the World' as its territory to avoid any breach of the licence.

Define the Product carefully and also include the price at which the Product is initially being sold. If the agreement is with the manufacturer, then you are talking about wholesale prices and you should ensure that the manufacturer can't sell the product retail or by mail order at a higher price or, alternatively, if they do, then the royalty will be based upon that.

The Term (Period) of the Agreement is going to be important because there may be an important sporting event coming up in which you hope your client will participate and which will put up his potential value.

You will grant the right to the manufacturer on a non-exclusive basis. Offer to be exclusive as far as the particular product is concerned but if you don't narrow that down, then you will find the manufacturer trying to be clever and saying you can't grant similar rights to anybody, even if the product concerned is non-competitive.

You will give the manufacturer the right to reproduce the name and image of your client in respect of the product but you also want to insert an obligation on the manufacturer to develop the product and actually market it. You may well get a substantial advance but the real profit is going to come from huge sales and there is no point in the whole lot lying on a shelf gathering dust.

Put an obligation on the manufacturer to promote and market the licensed item and try and set out the parameters of the money that they intend spending on the advertising campaign. Try and get a certain number of free samples for yourself and your client because you may be able to use them for charitable purposes. Don't let the manufacturer enter into any advertising campaign or promotions without you having copy control over everything that is being used. Put an obligation on the manufacturer to tell you if they come across any potential infringements of the trademark because the Trading Standards Officers may well bring them to their attention before yours.

Generally, what you are going to look for is an advance as well as some commission. The advance basically means money up front and can either be recoupable or non-recoupable. So what does that mean? You may well say, on behalf of your client, that you want a guaranteed sum of money just to enter into the licence, which has no relevance whatsoever to the number of items being sold. After that you want – say – anywhere between 8 and 12% of the wholesale price of the items by way of royalty. (I am using the words royalty and commission interchangeably although there are some good tax reasons why you should prefer to use the word royalty.) What is more normal is for the advance to be paid on account of commission and to be recoupable. Let's say that you get an advance of £20,000 and the royalty rate is 10%. That would mean that, until £200,000 worth of goods has been sold, your client doesn't get any more money, but after that he gets 10% of everything.

Make sure that the manufacturer doesn't get clever and try and slip in the word 'returnable' rather than 'recoupable' because that means that if the product is unsuccessful, they could come along and ask for their money back.

Ask to see details of all sales, including computer printouts and if it is a one-product company ask for copies of VAT returns. The same principles apply to inspections of accounts as I have set out before.

Make sure that the fact that you bank the cheques doesn't mean that you have necessarily accepted the figures. If the manufacturer does run a mixed business, then make sure they are obliged to keep separate records and accounts in respect of the manufacture and sale of the products concerning your client and to keep all their relevant invoice books and records for at least two years after the agreement has expired.

Before the product hits the market, you want to see it and you therefore need to receive samples and ensure that the product at all times accords with the sample. Restrain the manufacturer from cross-marketing the product, i.e. selling it in association with another product that your client has not been paid to endorse and, similarly, stop them from promoting the product through any newspaper without your consent. Your client may have a contract with one paper whilst the manufacturer wants to promote the product through another.

If there are any breaches of your intellectual property rights, let the manufacturer contract to join in with any proceedings and, if the breach is their fault, put in a clause saying that they have to pick up the costs.

Insert the appropriate provisions for termination. For example, if they have failed to promote and manufacture the product within a certain period of time, failed to give you the statements, failed to pay you the money or failed to comply with the sample. Obviously, you also want to be able to end the agreement if the manufacturer hits financial problems and has a Receiver appointed or is subject to a winding-up order.

At the end of the agreement, allow the manufacturer a 'run-off' period of, say, three months but after that get them to return all the stock to you or donate it to a suitable charity. You may enter into an agreement with somebody else for a similar product and you don't want your old manufacturer saturating the market with an old version of the product that they are trying to dump cheaply.

Stop the manufacturer assigning the benefit of the agreement. It may be that it becomes so successful that they think they could sell the benefit at a premium and there is no reason why you should find yourself licensed to another company with whom you could have negotiated more money.

On the subject of negotiating monies, how do you actually pitch for that? Well, the way to do it is to ask the manufacturer how many items of the product they think they will sell. Inevitably, they will go overboard because they want to try to persuade you to grant them the licence. At that point, work out how much your client would receive by way of royalties and that should be your starting point in respect of your advance. The argument for this is that if the manufacturer is so confident that they will sell those products, why should they be worried about giving you an advance? As I see it, that's where you start from but be prepared to discount that figure by as much as 50% because that should still give you a comfortable capital sum with which to benefit your client and to earn yourself your commission.

Also, don't forget that if you or a connected party acts for a footballer in his commercial matters that now means that even if you don't represent him on his playing contracts, even if you have never acted for him on his playing contracts, that you can't act for a club which wishes to sign him under The FA Regulations. It is absolutely absurd, particularly where the player has always had a totally different agent looking after his playing career. But there you go. If you work in Wonderland then you have to play along with Alice.

This brief summary of the licence isn't exhaustive but, hopefully, it gives you some of the more important bullet points so you can go out into the market place and beat up the innocent and unwary and make your client a richer and happier person.

Sponsorship and Endorsements

As a matter of practicality, I have had to be selective in relation to the commercial opportunities available to a sportsperson and the final port of call is going to be sponsorship. This differs from licensing insofar as a substantial sports company is seeking to get your client associated with all of its products and to use him or her as its public face for all potential customers.

Here the rewards can be far higher, as indeed can the obligations. It is highly unlikely that such an opportunity will come along unless you act for somebody in the top class of their sport. However, if you do, it is absolutely essential you get it right first time because you won't get a second opportunity. Also be careful in the case of a client who is part of a team at a club that you are not giving away any rights that have already been given away to the club in his playing contract. Remind yourself of what you have to negotiate with before you sit down to talk to the sponsor to ensure you don't make a terrible mistake. The same, of course, applies to licensing and indeed any commercial deals.

Once again, for the purposes of the agreement, many of the elements discussed in relation to the licence are relevant (parties, term, definitions, payment etc) but this time you will be defining a whole bunch of products rather than one single product. What you have to balance is the fact that you are taking your client out of the market place for all of those products and, given the size of the sponsor, there is no guarantee that they are actually going to make the product immediately for which they are securing the rights on day one. For example, a sports manufacturing company may want to secure your player's rights in relation to sunglasses or cosmetics, even though they only have blueprint plans for manufacturing or developing the particular ranges.

It is even more important when dealing with a document of this stature to keep in mind that the term must have some relation to forthcoming major sporting events though, quite frankly, from the sponsor's point of view, they are going to want to secure the rights for as long as possible if they are paying substantial monies.

This sort of agreement may well contain an item called 'signature products'. Quite simply, this means a boot or a tracksuit or even a ball or a pair of gloves with your client's signature on it. You should be seeking a separate advance in relation to these items and also a higher royalty rate because sales are clearly identifiable as having been generated by your client.

If a company is using your client to promote an existing product, then you should be asking for details of current sales and seeking a higher royalty on the uplift of those sales which you could reasonably argue has been generated by the use of your client's name, image, likeness, etc.

Certainly, as far as the signature products are concerned, don't forget to get an indemnity from the sponsors. By way of example, if they were to produce a signature shin-guard which fractured upon contact, there is every likelihood that your client will be sued as having induced the young buyer to purchase it because they are a famous sportsperson and have tacitly approved the quality of the same.

You will find that the personal obligations are far greater on your client. They will be expected to wear their sponsor's products whenever they attend any matches, attend training sessions, appear in interviews or engage in sports or sports products promotional activities. You must of course qualify this by saying that where their club insists on them wearing something different, they won't be obliged to wear the sponsor's product. Similarly, it won't be unreasonable for the sponsor to expect your client to use reasonable endeavours to wear and promote the products even in respect of general interest interviews and photographs. Again, seek a complete exclusion in relation to any obligations arising both from club and country.

There will be a wide obligation to act as a promoter of the sponsoring company and the product and to assist in product development and testing new products. There is no doubt there will be a fair amount of haggling over the number of appearances and, when substantial monies are involved, these can be as many as a dozen personal appearances in a year. I have already mentioned how carefully you need to define personal appearances and this is even more the case in a contract of this nature, where your client can be expected to be flown abroad to promote the sponsor company and the product. This may involve sports clinics, coaching courses, sports or leisurewear exhibitions, conferences, trade fairs, promotional launches, in-store appearances, posing for photographs, posters, promotional videos or other advertising media. You should specifically exclude or negotiate special terms for TV advertisements although whether or not these are to be included will depend upon the amount of the advance that is being paid to your client.

There will be an obligation on the sponsor to provide free kit up to a certain value to the client and you should try to extend this so that it is not just for their personal use. Sportspeople, being who they are, will almost certainly want kit for their friends and family. Try and get the base figure uplifted over the period of the contract, say in proportion to the increase in sales of the product. In any event, always ensure that you can buy additional items at wholesale prices (and that should be 'best' wholesale).

Basically, for a contract of this nature, there should be three income streams: a retainer (i.e. the payment that procured your client to enter into the contract); the royalty or commission (into which I would tie the advance); and bonus payments. Bonus payments should be geared to international recognition and special sporting performances either at club or country level. If the player's club wins the Premiership or their rugby team wins the European Cup, there will be more interest focused upon the player. If the player individually covers himself with glory at club or international level, again that generates more interest for the player and more interest for the sponsor.

I have already dealt with accounting procedures in the licence and there is no real reason why they should differ for a contract of this nature although, because of the sums involved and the size of the sponsor, the policing may be a little more difficult.

If there are to be signature products, then ensure there is an obligation to develop, distribute and sell the products and, in particular, try and get an obligation to develop junior products with signatures because these are more likely to sell. It is a fact of life that children are more anxious to have their hero's signature on the boot they are wearing than adults.

The sponsor may be very concerned as to where your client is going to be performing his sporting obligations. They may have done a deal with them at, say, Manchester United but might be less interested if they were to move to, say, Real Madrid because they are not very strong in Spain. From your point of view, you would be arguing that your client is an international in the public eye and the sponsor will receive as much exposure wherever he plays. You might compromise by agreeing in advance which clubs in which countries would have no impact on the deal, which would increase the deal and which clubs or countries would reduce it.

As far as termination is concerned, as well as those clauses set out previously, there would probably be a 'morality' clause inserted because sponsors are notoriously sensitive about criminal convictions, drink, drugs and bad tabloid headlines. They will almost certainly want to insert a clause saying that if your client retires from sport, then the agreement can be terminated but quite often there is life after retirement in endorsing a company's products and it may be possible to negotiate an alternate deal based upon their career in the media.

Similarly, the sponsor may want to include a clause saying they can terminate in the event that your client is injured for a long time and whenever the word 'injury' crops up, the word 'insurance' should flash up in letters a mile high. If you don't insure your client and he gets injured and his major sponsor terminates, you are throwing yourself wide open to a negligence action.

With regard to termination, include the same run-off provision to which I referred in the licence. You will probably encounter resistance, but try and exclude one-off promotions in the newspaper to which your client is contracted. If they decide to issue a commemorative T-shirt which will have massive sales, assuming your client has done something magnificent on the pitch, you don't want them to be stopped from doing this by the fact that you have a sponsorship deal with a clothing manufacturing company.

One area I have not previously mentioned concerns rights of first dealing and first refusal. In America the whole concept of the 'right to match' is very popular. What this means is that, towards the end of the contract, if you get an offer from a rival manufacturer for your client's services, you have to give his existing sponsor the right to match it. That means disclosing to the existing sponsor all the details of the new deal that is on the table which, personally, I find offensive and resist at every opportunity. However, a right of 'first dealing' is perfectly reasonable. It simply means that, for example, in the last six months of the contract, you and the sponsor can sit down and discuss whether there is to be a renewal and upon what terms.

So much to explain, so little space, but there you have it. I have taken you from the situation where you have decided to set up in business, explained how to get clients, how you negotiate for them and how you earn your money. Being a sports agent is a bit like life – you can't really learn about it from reading books, you have to live it. So you are out there now, you're on your own and all I can say is, 'Good luck and enjoy it'. There's no point in doing anything in life if you don't enjoy it. Oh, and by the way, I'd be grateful if you don't try to pinch any of my clients.

Useful Addresses

The Lawn Tennis Association, The Queens Club, Palliser Road, West Kensington, London W14 9EG.
Tel 020 7381 7000
http://www.lta.org.uk

The Rugby Football Union, Twickenham Stadium, Rugby Road, Twickenham, Middx TW1 1DZ.
Tel 020 8891 4565 Fax 020 8744 2104
http://www.rfu.com

The England and Wales Cricket Board (ECB), c/o Lord's Cricket Club, St John's Wood, London NW8 8QN.
Tel 020 7432 1200
http://www.ecb.co.uk

The International Cricket Conference http://www.icc-cricket.com

The Football Association, 25 Soho Square, London W1D 4FA.
Tel 020 7745 4545 Fax 020 7745 4646
http://www.the-fa.org

The Scottish FA, Hampden Park, Glasgow G42 9AY
Tel 0141 616 6000

FIFA, PO Box 85, 8030 Zurich, Switzerland.
Tel 0041 1 384 9595 Fax 00 41 1 384 9696
http://www.fifa.com

The Premier League, 30 Gloucester Place, London, W1U 8PL
Tel 0207 298 1600

The Football League, 5, Edward VII Quay, Navigation Way, Preston, Lancs.
Tel 01772 325801

The Football Conference, Third Floor, Wellington House, 31–34 Waterloo Street, Birmingham B2 5TJ
Tel 0121 2141950

UEFA (Union of European Football Association) Route de Geneve, 46, Case Postale, CH-1260, Nyon, Switzerland.
Tel 00 41 22 994 44 44

The British Boxing Board of Control, The Old Library, Trinity Street, Cardiff, CF10 1BH

King's College, London (Postgraduate Certificate in Sports Law), Strand, London, WC2R 2LS

PGA, Centenary House, The Belfry, Sutton Coldfield, West Midlands, B76 9PT

USA Addresses and Contacts

Paul Tagliabue, Commissioner, National Football League, 280 Park Avenue, New York, NY 10017
Tel (212) 450-2000
www.nfl.com

David Stern, Commissioner, National Basketball Association, 645 Fifth Avenue, New York, NY 10022
Tel (212) 826-7000

Gary Bettman, Commissioner, National Hockey League, 1251 Avenue of the Americas, New York, NY 10020
Tel (212) 789-2000

Allan H. (Bud) Selig, Commissioner, Major League Baseball, 245 Park Avenue, 31st Floor, New York, NY 10167
Tel (212) 931-7800

Don Garber, Commissioner, Major League Soccer, 110 East 42nd Street, 10th Floor New York, New York 10017
Tel (212) 450-1200

Appendices

For the latest version of The Football Association Agents Regulations please go to:

http://www.thefa.com/TheFA/RulesAndRegulations/Agents/
Postings/2007/09/NewAgentsRegulations.htm

For the latest version of the FIFA Players Agent Regulations please go to:

http://www.fifa.com/aboutfifa/federation/administration/
playersagents/regulations.html

STANDARD REPRESENTATION AGREEMENT

<u>REPRESENTATION CONTRACT between AGENT and PLAYER</u>

THIS REPRESENTATION CONTRACT is made the   day of

BETWEEN

[NAME OF INDIVIDUAL AUTHORISED AGENT] (the 'Authorised Agent')

[LICENCE / REGISTRATION NUMBER] of

[COMPANY NAME and ADDRESS (where applicable)] (the 'Company')

and

[THE PLAYER]

[ADDRESS]

(D.O.B).

1.   The Authorised Agent has informed the Player in writing that he should consider taking independent legal advice in relation to this Representation Contract and he has afforded the Player the opportunity to take such legal advice prior to the execution of this Representation Contract.

2.   The Player has provided written confirmation in the form set out at Appendix 1 to this Representation Contract on or before the date of this Representation Contract that either:

(a)   he has obtained such legal advice; or

(b)   he has decided he does not need to do so.

3.   **APPOINTMENT**

The Player hereby appoints the Authorised Agent to provide The Services as hereinafter defined on the following terms as hereinafter contained subject to the provisions of the Football Association Football Agents Regulations (hereinafter called "The Agents' Regulations).

4.   **THE SERVICES**

The Authorised Agent shall represent The Player in relation to all income producing activities whatsoever and wheresoever arising from the Player's occupation as a professional footballer including but not limited to the negotiation of all professional playing contracts with football clubs and the procurement of clubs for The Player for The Player within The Agents

Regulations and the sourcing and procurement and negotiation of all commercial contracts for The Player and the development and marketing of The Player's image.

5.   **TERM**

The Term of this Representation Contract shall, subject to clauses 14 - 17 below, be for a period of two years from the date hereof at the end of which it shall terminate without notice. The Representation Contract may be renewed at any time upon the written agreement of both parties, provided that the Term of the Representation Contract renewed by the parties shall not be for a term of more than 2 years.

6.   **REMUNERATION**

(A)   In consideration of the provision of the Services, the Player shall pay to the Authorised Agent a fee in accordance with the requirements The Agents Regulations and the terms of this Representation Contract as follows:

(a)   a commission of five per cent (5%) of the annual gross guaranteed salary (signing on fees and basic salary from time to time) payable to the Player and arising from any contract with any club negotiated by the Agent (or by the Player himself during the Term).

The payment shall be made by way of a lump sum payment at the start of the Player's playing contract in respect of the period from the date of signing until the 30th June following and thereafter on:

(b)   1 July of each year of the Playing Contract during the Term;

OR

(c)   an annual payment on 30 June of each year of the Player's contract;

OR

(b)   a monthly payment:

(ii)   made by the Player's club at the direction of the Player; or
(iii)   made by the Player on the 30th day of each month.

OR

(c)   a lump sum payment at the start of the Player's Playing Contract in relation to the entire gross value of the Contract.

OR

(d)   A periodical lump sum payment to coincide with the receipt by the Player of each instalment of his signing on fee or if no signing on fee is payable an annual lump sum payment commencing on the date of execution of the playing contract negotiated by the Agent and thereafter on each anniversary of the said playing contract.

[DELETE WHICHEVER OF THE ABOVE DO NOT APPLY]

(B) The above sums are exclusive of any Value Added Tax that may be payable.

(C) Payment of the sums due above shall be made subject to receipt by the Player of the Authorised Agent's or The Company's written invoices therefor.

(D) If The Player makes a written request pursuant to Clause 9(f) of this Agreement and concludes a professional playing contract without utilising the services of The Authorised Agent he shall still be obliged to make the payment referred to in clause 6(A) hereof.

EXCLUSIVITY

7. The Parties agree that this Agreement is exclusive and the Player shall not be entitled to appoint any other Authorised Agent, as defined in the Agents Regulations to provide any Services agreed to be provided by the Agent hereunder.

OBLIGATIONS

8. The Authorised Agent undertakes and warrants to the Player that he will at all times during the term of this Representation Contract perform the Services conscientiously and in the best interests of the Player and, in particular:

    (a) he shall provide the Services to the best of his ability and use all reasonable endeavours in connection therewith. It is agreed and accepted that no guarantee is given as to the actual procurement of any such activities or opportunities as referred to in clause 4 hereof;

    (b). he shall keep the Player informed of any and all material information relating to the provision of the Services and shall not enter into negotiations with any third parties on the Player's behalf without the Player's consent;

    (c) he shall comply with the Rules of the Football Association and the Agents Regulations;

    (d) he holds, and will continue to hold, a current valid licence/registration issued by The Football Association;

    (e) he has, and shall maintain, in place valid and effective professional liability insurance in respect of the Services and shall, at the Player's request, provide the Player with a copy of the policy;

    (f) he shall not, either directly or indirectly, make payments of any kind to, or receive payments of any kind from, a Club (as defined in the Agents Regulations), which results from the provision of the Services, save where permitted in accordance with the Agents Regulations;

    (g) he shall not incur any liability in excess of £1000 on behalf of the Player without the prior consent of the Player;

(h)   he shall, on or before 30 September each year, provide an itemised statement (in the form prescribed by The Football Association from time to time) to the Player covering the period from 1 July of the previous year to 30 June of the relevant year, which sets out any and all remuneration or payments of whatever nature, including in relation to Commercial Rights (as defined in the Agents Regulations), charged by the Authorised Agent to the Player during that period.

9.   The Player undertakes and warrants to the Authorised Agent that:

(a)   he is free to enter into the Representation Contract and is not prevented or restricted from so doing by any other extant agreement with another authorised agent or otherwise;

(b)   he shall notify the Authorised Agent of any approach or offer or enquiry that the Player receives from any other authorised agent, club or person acting directly or indirectly on behalf of a club that falls within the scope of the Services. The Player shall not be entitled to engage the services of another authorised agent without the prior written consent of the Authorised Agent;

(c)   he shall comply with the Rules of the Football Association and the Agents Regulations;

(d)   he will enter into and to the best of his ability carry out the terms of any agreement negotiated on his behalf with his consent and authority by the Authorised Agent and indemnify the Authorised Agent in relation to any breach thereof.

(e)   he shall provide any such information that the Authorised Agent may reasonably require in order to enable the Authorised Agent to perform the Services hereunder; and

(f)   where permitted by this Representation Contract, if he makes a written request to a club that the club deal with someone other than the Authorised Agent, including with the Player himself, in relation to a Transaction or Contract Negotiation (as defined within the Agents Regulations) he shall provide the Authorised Agent with a copy of the written request as soon as reasonably practical and in any event within 5 days of its execution and shall also provide the Authorised Agent with a copy of any agreement entered into by The Player during The Term where The Player has not utilised the Services of the Authorised Agent and as soon as reasonably practical and in any event within 5 days of the execution of such agreement

10.   The Player shall not be obliged to use the Services of the Authorised Agent during the term of this Representation Contract and may represent himself in any Transaction or Contract Negotiation (as defined in the Agents Regulations) should he so desire subject to the provisions of clause 6(D) and 9(f) hereof.

11.   In the event of any payment due from the Player to the Agent not being paid on the due date it shall bear interest at a rate of 3% above Barclays Base Rate for the time being.

12.   [The Player also appoints the Agent to represent him exclusively in relation to all income producing activities and opportunities outside of his Playing Contract which are or may

become available to the Player in any part of the world arising from the Player's career as a footballer and from his name, image and reputation (the "Commercial Rights"). In respect of the Commercial Rights the Agent shall be entitled to charge a fee of 20% plus VAT of the gross income arising therefrom whether during or after the expiry of the Term.]

DELETE IF THIS DOES NOT APPLY

13. In relation to payments due pursuant to the Playing Contract the Player shall remain obliged to continue payments to the Authorised Agent as set out above after the expiry of the Term subject to the provisions of the Agents Regulations.

TERMINATION

14. If the Authorised Agent's licence/registration is suspended or withdrawn during the term of this Representation Contract as determined by The Football Association or other relevant national association or FIFA, and the relevant appeal process has been exhausted where applicable, then this Representation Contract shall be automatically terminated with immediate effect.

15. If either party:

(a) commits a material breach of this Representation Contract which is not capable of remedy;

(b). commits a material breach of this Representation Contract which is capable of being remedied but fails to remedy such breach within 30 days of a receipt of written notice from the non-defaulting party specifying the breach and requiring it to be remedied; or

(c) is declared bankrupt [or, in the case of the Authorised Agent only, if the Company becomes insolvent], this Representation Contract may be terminated by the non-defaulting party on written notice with immediate effect.

16. Any sums that fall due for payment to the Authorised Agent after termination of this Representation Contract, other than those sums arising out of rights that have been accrued before termination, shall not be due and payable by the Player if:

(a). the Representation Contract is terminated in accordance with clause 14; or

(b). the Representation Contract is terminated in accordance with clause 15 to the extent only that the material breach giving rise to such termination is committed by the Authorised Agent.

17. [WHERE THE AUTHORISED AGENT IS EMPLOYED OR RETAINED ON BEHALF OF AN ORGANISATION - Should the Authorised Agent, during the term of this Representation Contract, cease to be an employee or director or other authorised representative of the Company, the Player shall be informed in writing by the Authorised Agent as soon as reasonably practicable thereafter, and the Player shall be given the option to:

(a) continue to be represented by the Authorised Agent under this Representation Contract subject to any provisions, restrictions or obligations that may exist between the Authorised Agent and the Company; or

(b)   terminate the Representation Contract and be represented by, and enter into a representation contract with, another authorised agent employed by the Company without any further obligations to the Authorised Agent other than in respect of any outstanding sums that are or shall be due to the Authorised Agent hereunder (subject to the relevant provisions of the Agents Regulations regarding entitlement to remuneration and to any provisions or obligations that may exist between the Authorised Agent and the Company); or

(c)   terminate the Representation Contract and, if he so wishes, seek alternative representation without any further obligations to the Authorised Agent and/or the Company other than in respect of any outstanding sums that are or shall be due to the Authorised Agent hereunder (subject to the relevant provisions of the Agents Regulations regarding entitlement to remuneration and any provisions or obligations that may exist between the Authorised Agent and the Company).

(d)   The Player shall be required to notify the Authorised Agent in writing of his election within 28 days of receiving notice from the Authorised Agent of his change in circumstances, and in the event that the Player elects the option set out in clause 17(b) above, the Authorised Agent shall sign any documents and do any acts as may be necessary to novate this Representation Contract to a third party authorised agent employed by the Company.]

NOTICES

18.   All notices to be given under this Representation Contract shall be in writing in English and left at or sent by first class registered or recorded delivery mail or facsimile to the address of the party as set out above or to such other address and/or addresses as the party concerned shall from time to time designate by written notice pursuant hereto.

19.   Any such notice shall be deemed given, in the case of hand delivery, at the time when the same is left at the addressee's address or, in the case of first class registered post or recorded delivery mail, on the business day after delivery or, in the case of a facsimile, upon transmission by the sender provided that the transmitting facsimile machine generates upon completion of the transmission a transmission report stating that the notice has been duly transmitted without error to the addressee's facsimile number.

SEVERABILITY

20.   If any term or provision in this Representation Contract shall be held to be illegal, invalid or unenforceable, in whole or part, under any enactment or rule of law, such term or provision or part shall to that extent be deemed not to form part of this Representation Contract but the legality, validity and enforceability of the remainder of this Representation Contract shall not be affected.

CONFIDENTIALITY

21.   Save as required by law or any fiscal or regulatory authority (including The Football Association), each party undertakes to keep the terms of this Representation Contract and any information of a confidential nature that he may receive in respect of the other party during the term of this Representation Contract strictly confidential and shall at no time (whether before or after expiry of the term of this Representation Contract) divulge any such

information to any third party (other than to their respective professional advisors) without the consent of the other party.

ENTIRE AGREEMENT

22. This Representation Contract sets out the entire agreement between the parties hereto, in relation to those matters set out herein, and supersedes all prior discussions statements representations and undertakings between them or their advisors.

23. Clause 22 shall not exclude any liability which either party would otherwise have to the other or any right which either of them may have to rescind this Representation Contract in respect of any statements made fraudulently by the other prior to the execution of this Representation Contract or any rights which either of them may have in respect of fraudulent concealment by the other.

24. This Representation Contract may not be amended, modified or superseded unless expressly agreed to in writing by both parties with such amended agreement being lodged with The Football Association within 5 days of execution.

RELATIONSHIP BETWEEN THE PARTIES

25. The Authorised Agent is not authorised under this Representation Contract to enter into employment contracts on behalf of the Player or bind the Player in a contractual relationship in any way whatsoever, [save as provided for under Clause 8(g)].

SURVIVAL OF RIGHTS, DUTIES AND OBLIGATIONS

26. Expiry or termination of this Representation Contract shall not release the parties from any liability or right of action or claim which at the time of such expiry or termination has already accrued or may accrue to either party in respect of any act or omission prior to such expiry or termination.

27. Expiry or termination shall not affect the coming into force or the continuance in force of any provision hereof which is expressly or by implication intended to come into or continue in force on or after such termination.

NON-ASSIGNMENT

28. The Authorised Agent shall not assign sub-contract or novate the benefit or burden of this Representation Agreement or any of its provisions without the prior consent in writing of the Player (such consent to be given or withheld in the Player's absolute discretion) and in any case shall not assign sub-contract or novate the benefit or burden of its Representation Contract or any of its provisions to an unauthorised agent as defined in the Agents Regulation and any such assignment shall be subject to The Football Association Agents Regulations then in force.

THIRD PARTY RIGHTS

29. Notwithstanding any other provision of this Representation Contract, a person who is not a party to this Representation Contract has no rights under the Contracts (Rights of Third

Parties) Acts 1999 or otherwise to rely upon or enforce any term of this Representation Contract.

SUPPLEMENTAL AGREEMENTS

30.   Any other arrangements between the parties in any way connected to the provision of the Services that are supplemental to this Representation Contract shall be in accordance with the requirements of the Agents' Regulations and shall be annexed to the Representation Contract and submitted to The Football Association (and other relevant national association) for registration together with this Representation Contract.

DISPUTES

31.   Any dispute between the parties arising from this Representation Contract which constitutes a breach of the Rules of the Football Association Rules and/or the Agents Regulations shall be dealt with by the Rules of the Football Association in the first instance and referred to FIFA where appropriate. Any other dispute between the parties shall be dealt with as between the parties under Rule K (Arbitration) of the Rules of the Football Association (as may be varied from time to time).

GOVERNING LAW & JURISDICTION

32.   This Representation Contract shall be construed and interpreted in accordance with the laws of England and Wales and, subject to clause 31 above, the parties hereby submit to the exclusive jurisdiction of the courts of England and Wales.

SIGNATURES

This contract has been signed in fivefold and the copies have been distributed to:

i.   The National Association with which the Authorised Agent is registered
ii.   The National Association with which the Player is registered
iii.   The Authorised Agent/Registered Lawyer
iv.   The Player

Signed by the Player: _____   Date: _____

Print Name: _____

Signed by the Authorised Agent: _____   Date: _____

Signed by the Registered Lawyer: _____   Date: _____

REGISTRATION

The Football Association: _____ **Date:** _____

Other National Association: _____ **Date:** _____

Appendix 1

Independent Legal Advice Confirmation

I [insert player's name] confirm that I received independent legal advice from [Lawyer's name   ] of [name of firm] as to the terms and effect of this Representation Contract

I [insert player's name] confirm that I have been advised by [insert Authorised Agent's name] to consider taking independent legal advice in relation to the terms of this Representation Contract, and that I have been given a reasonable opportunity to take such independent legal advice, but that I have decided that I do not need to do so.

Signed by the Player: _____   Date: _____

Print Name: _____

Index